GOD
WITH
US

Light for Your Path

The Light for Your Path Series is for women who desire to know, love, and serve God better. Each book is designed to nurture new believers while challenging women who are ready for deeper study. Studies in the series examine *books* of the Bible, on the one hand (look for subtitles beginning with *Light from*), and important *topics* in Christian faith and life, on the other (look for subtitles beginning with *Focus on*). The series blends careful instruction with active reader participation in a variety of study exercises, always encouraging women to live in the light of biblical truth in practical ways.

Two foundational studies explain why and how to study the Bible as the one perfect light source for your Christian walk:

A Book Like No Other: What's So Special About the Bible
Turning On the Light: Discovering the Riches of God's Word

Also available:

The Light for Your Path Series Leader's Guide

GOD
WITH
US

*Light from
the Gospels*

Carol J. Ruvolo

P&R
PUBLISHING
P.O. BOX 817 • PHILLIPSBURG • NEW JERSEY 08865-0817

Printed in the United States of America

Composition by Colophon Typesetting
Cover design by Now You See it!

Library of Congress Cataloging-in-Publication Data

Ruvolo, Carol J., 1946–
    God with us : light from the Gospels / Carol J. Ruvolo.
       p.   cm. — (Light for your path)
    Includes bibliographical references (p.)
    ISBN 0-87552-629-2 (pbk.)
    1. Bible. N.T. Gospels—Study and teaching. 2. Women—Religious life.   I. Title. II. Series.
BS2556.R88   1998
226´.0071—dc21   98–20122

To Blair Willis

One of life's most precious treasures,
a true and trusted friend.

CONTENTS

Contents

The Light for Your Path Series

The Light for Your Path Series is designed to help women learn how to glorify and enjoy God by living out their transformation in Jesus Christ. Each book in the series reflects the author's commitment to the Bible as the infallible, inerrant, authoritative, and entirely sufficient Word of God, and her conviction that Reformed theology is the clearest and most accurate restatement of biblical truth.

The series begins with two foundational studies centering on the Bible itself. *A Book Like No Other: What's So Special About the Bible* presents (in six lessons) the unique character of God's revelation. *Turning On the Light: Discovering the Riches of God's Word* provides (in seven lessons) an effective approach to studying the Bible. Combining these two books in a thirteen-week course will prepare new and veteran students to gain the most from the Light for Your Path Series.

The remaining studies in the series fall into two categories. "Light" studies cover particular *books* of the Bible (or sections of books, or groups of books such as the Gospels). These studies guide you through portions of Scripture, enabling you to understand and apply the meaning of each passage. You will recognize them by their subtitles, beginning with the words *Light from*.

"Focus" studies spotlight important *topics* in the Christian faith and life, such as prayer, salvation, righteousness, and relationships, and seek to show what the whole Bible says about them. These studies also stress understanding and applying biblical truth in daily life. Their subtitles begin with the words *Focus on*. Studying a combination of biblical books and topics will shed much-needed scriptural light on your walk with God. Both types of Bible study should be included in a "balanced diet" for a growing Christian.

The *Leader's Guide* that accompanies this series contains a complete description of the purpose and format of these studies, along with helpful suggestions for leading women through them.

Bible study is a serious task that involves a significant investment of time and energy. Preparing yourself to study effectively will help you reap the greatest benefit from that investment. Study when you are well rested and alert. Try to find a time and place that is quiet, free of distractions, and conducive to concentration. Use a loose-leaf or spiral notebook to take notes on what you read and to do the exercises in this study. You may also want to develop a simple filing system so that you can refer to these notes in later studies.

Approach Bible study as you would any task that requires thought and effort to do well. Don't be surprised if it challenges you and stretches your thinking. Expect it to be difficult at times but extremely rewarding.

Always begin your study with prayer. Ask the Lord to reveal sin in your life that needs to be confessed and cleansed, to help you concentrate on His truths, and to illumine your mind with understanding of what He has written. End your study with a prayer for opportunities to apply what you have learned and wisdom to recognize those opportunities when they occur.

Each lesson in these studies is followed by three types of "Exercises": "Review," "Application," and "Digging Deeper." The *review* exercises will help you determine how well you understood the lesson material by giving you an opportunity to express the key points in your own words. The *application* exercises encourage you to put your understanding of the material to work in your daily life. And the *digging deeper* exercises challenge you to pursue further study in certain key areas.

You should be able to find the answers to the *review* questions in the lesson material itself, but please resist the temptation to copy words or phrases out of the lesson when you answer these questions. Work at putting these ideas into your own words. When you can do this, you know you have understood what you have read. It might help to ask yourself, "How would I explain this idea to someone else if I didn't have the book with me?"

If you don't have time to do all of the *application* exercises, pray over them and ask the Lord to show you which one(s) *He* wants you to work on. Because you will be applying the lessons to your daily life, these applications should take some time and thought. Answering one of them well will benefit you more than answering all of them superficially.

Answers to the application exercises should be very specific. Work at avoiding vague generalities. It might help to keep in mind that a specific application will answer the questions Who? What? When? Where? and How? A vague generality will not. You can make applications in the areas of your thinking, your attitudes, and your behavior. (See lesson 6 of *Turning On the Light* for more about application.)

Digging deeper exercises usually require a significant amount of time and effort to complete. They were designed to provide a challenge for mature Christians who are eager for more advanced study. However, new Christians should not automatically pass them by. The Holy Spirit may choose to use one of them to help you grow. Remember that *all Christians* grow by stretching beyond where they are right now. So if one or two of these exercises intrigue you, spend some time working on them. And, do not hesitate to ask for help from your pastor, elders, or more mature Christian friends.

As you work through this study, resist the temptation to compare yourself with other Christians in your group. The purpose of this study is to help you grow in your faith by learning and applying God's truth in your daily life—not to fill up a study book with brilliantly worded answers. If you learn and apply *one element* of God's truth in each lesson, you are consistently moving beyond where you were when you began.

Always remember that effective Bible study equips you *to glorify God and enjoy Him forever.* You glorify God when you live in such a way that those around you can look at you and see an accurate reflection of God's character and nature. You enjoy God when you are fully satisfied in His providential ordering of the circumstances in your life. When your life glorifies God and your joy is rooted in His providence, your impact on our fallen world will be tremendous.

A man who was merely a man
and said the sort of things Jesus said
would not be a great moral teacher.
He would either be a lunatic—
on a level with the man who says he is a poached egg—
or else he would be the Devil of Hell.
You must make your choice.
Either this man was, and is, the Son of God:
or else a madman or something worse.
You can shut Him up for a fool,
you can spit at Him and kill Him as a demon;
or you can fall at His feet and call Him Lord and God.
But let us not come with any patronizing nonsense
about His being a great human teacher.
He has not left that open to us.
He did not intend to.
—C. S. Lewis

The Beginning

(The stranger, the Jew, and the other characters in this story are fictitious. However, the events surrounding Jesus' crucifixion that serve as its backdrop are historical facts. You may read about them in the Gospels, written by Matthew, Mark, Luke, and John.)

*J*ERUSALEM, NISAN, A.D. 30: *The stranger cast an apprehensive glance at Jerusalem's darkening sky and quickened his steps. He had not planned to be here at Passover, but his capricious gods had obviously decreed otherwise. From the looks of things this morning, they were still conspiring against him.*

The streets were clogged with excited, chattering people. An unconventional predawn trial had brought them out early to watch the show and discuss the conviction. Snatches of impassioned conversation floated around the disgruntled stranger as he fought his way through the nearly impassable streets.

"Jesus, the Rabbi from Nazareth . . ." ". . . condemned . . ." ". . . tried Him at night." "Cowards." "One of His own men turned Him in . . ." ". . . a good man . . ." ". . . in league with Satan . . ." ". . . healed my daughter . . ." "He said He was God." ". . . a blasphemer . . ." ". . . healed my mother . . ." ". . . raised a dead man . . ." "Can He raise Himself?"

It was getting darker. The stranger cursed. A storm brewing—another delay. He looked up and stood still. Not a cloud in the sky, and no sign of a storm. Only darkness—at midday.

"What is it?" A frightened woman asked everyone's question.

"Let's go." Her husband jerked her arm and their child began to cry. The sky was now completely black, unbroken by a single star. The stranger stood frozen, transfixed by the strange sight.

"Do not be afraid, my friend." A tall, muscular Jew touched the stranger's arm and gestured toward a low doorway. "We can wait there until it passes."

The stranger stepped away from the Jew. "Who are you? What is happening?"

"I am a friend," the Jew said quietly. "And I will not harm you. Come."

The doorway opened into a small garden. The Jew sat on a narrow stone bench barely visible in the gloom. "Please join me. We may be here awhile."

"Who are you? Do you know what's happening?" The stranger lingered near the doorway.

"I am a Jew—a follower of the one who was tried and condemned this morning."

"You are a criminal!"

"I am not a criminal." The gentle words drifted through the darkness, their sincerity convincing. "And neither was the Rabbi. Please stay with me. You cannot run in this darkness, and I would like to tell you His story."

The stranger perched lightly on the edge of the bench, poised for flight at a moment's notice.

The Jew's story was long, but oddly enthralling. The stranger's tenseness gradually melted away as he listened. Something in him desperately wanted to believe what he was hearing.

Suddenly an anguished cry ripped through the darkness. The stranger stiffened as icy shivers cascaded down his spine. He saw the Jew was fully alert, breathing quickly, listening as the cry's echoes gave way to a terrifying roar.

The ground around them began to tremble. The stranger covered his ears and fell to the ground. The Jew fell near him, curling around him in a protective embrace. Time stopped.

The stranger lay still. Slowly he realized the ground was no longer moving, and the roar had dissolved into an eerie silence. He lifted his head and opened his eyes. Light was returning to the sky.

The Jew was sitting next to him, head bowed between his knees, shoulders heaving with wrenching sobs.

Gently, the stranger touched the big man's arm. "Is it over?"

The Jew turned his tear-drenched face to the brightening sky, "Yes—and no," he said through a ragged sigh. "His work is done, but ours has only begun."

—   —   —

ALBUQUERQUE, DECEMBER 1998: Nancy tried to tune out the irreverently jazzy rendition of "Joy to the World!" blaring though the packed department store as her eyes skimmed mountains of gaudy gift ideas. "Housewares should be somewhere near that back wall. . . . Aha!" Spotting a glittery toaster display, she headed toward it.

"Nancy! Nancy! Is that you?"

The familiar voice belonged to her next-door neighbor, Mandy, whose familiar form suddenly broke free of a melee of shoppers attacking the perfume counter. "Hey, I thought that was you!" she exclaimed with a quick hug. "What are you doing here? I thought all your shopping was done."

"So did I—until last night. Then Jack reminded me that our niece is getting married on New Year's Eve. So here I am trying to find a wedding present."

"Oh, you poor thing! Have you had lunch? C'mon. I'll buy."

Ten minutes later, the two women settled into the cozy warmth of the third-floor coffee shop and pored over the enticing menu. "Well, it's turkey on wheat with no mayo for me," Nancy sighed. "With all the tasting and sampling I've done this year, I can hardly zip my jeans."

Mandy chuckled. "I know what you mean. I'll be eating salad till June."

After giving their orders to the harried waitress, Mandy relaxed against the cushioned booth and smiled. "You know, even though I get tired and gain weight and rush around like crazy, Christmas is my favorite time of year. No matter how hectic things get, people seem a little nicer somehow. My mother-in-law even sweetens up!" Nancy laughed. She didn't know her neighbor very well but had heard her mention difficulties with her husband's mother more than once.

"Well, I guess that's what Christmas is all about, huh?" Mandy continued. "Friends and family and goodwill and all that stuff. Don't you think so?"

Nancy's stomach knotted sharply. She had been praying for an opportunity to witness to Mandy, and suddenly, the door was wide open. *Lord, help me,* she prayed silently as she responded. "Actually no, I don't think that's what Christmas is all about. Would you like to hear why I celebrate Christmas?"

— — —

What *is* Christmas all about?

It's about a Crucifixion—and a Resurrection. It's about a man who was God—and why He lived—and died—and rose again. It's about hopeless sin, unique propitiation, and gracious forgiveness. It's about a life like no other—the life of Jesus Christ. His story is told in the Gospels, and that is the subject of our study.

The Gospels are the heart of God's revelation to us. They pump life through every page of Scripture while depending on those very pages for their ability to do so. The Gospels and the rest of Scripture exist in life-sustaining symbiosis. Neither makes sense without the other; and without each other, both would die.

Since our study is the Gospels, let's begin by examining their context, the bigger picture. It begins with God's creation of the heavens and the earth. He spoke the world into being, and formed a man from the dust of the ground. He breathed into him the breath of life, and man became a living soul, able to commune with God—but also able to sin.

God gave the man a simple command, and the man sinned by disobeying it. God responded by righteously cursing the man with death, and graciously promising him redemption.

Man's iniquity increased until only one righteous family was left. God destroyed the world with a catastrophic flood but saved that one family. Noah and his kin committed themselves to obedience, but their descendants failed to follow through. They disobeyed God's command to spread out and fill the earth, choosing instead to establish a local empire, marked by the mighty Tower of Babel. God intervened again to force their compliance. He halted their building project, confused their speech, and scattered them over the face of the earth.

Eventually, God called a man named Abram out of Ur of the Chaldees to father a nation through whom all the people of the earth would be blessed. God changed Abram's name to Abraham, meaning "father of a multitude," and renewed His covenant of redemption with him. The redeemer Messiah would spring from his line. Abraham believed God's promises and was declared righteous because of it.

God renewed His promise to Abraham's son, Isaac, and his grandson, Jacob. He changed Jacob's name to Israel and blessed him with twelve sons who founded twelve chosen tribes. The promised Redeemer would eventually come through Judah's tribe.

Eleven of those sons were jealous of their father's favorite, Joseph, and sold him into Egyptian slavery. They meant it for evil, but God used it for good. Establishing Joseph in a position of power, He used him to save the nation from starvation during an intense famine. Israel resided in Egypt 430 years, eventually becoming Pharaoh's slaves.

The burdens of God's people became more than they could bear, and they cried out to God for deliverance. God heard their cries and raised up Moses to deliver them. He revealed Himself to Moses by the name "I AM" and renewed the promise He had made to his fathers. He sent Moses, with miraculous power, to demand from Pharaoh his people's release. Once they were free, God gave them His law and the pattern for the tabernacle so that they would acknowledge their sin and worship in ways that pictured their coming Redeemer.

An unfaithful generation failed to appreciate and trust God's providential care, and they were wiped out in forty years of wilderness wanderings. God then appointed two faithful men, Joshua and Caleb, to lead a new generation into the Land of Promise.

During Joshua's life, the people faithfully served God, but following his death, they defected to idolatry. God delivered them into the hands of their enemies, but when they cried out to Him, He raised up judges to restore them. The people failed to learn, and this sorry cycle of sin, slavery, crying, and deliverance continued until the days of Samuel. Unhappy with their peculiar status, the people asked Samuel for a king so that they could be like their neighbors. God chastened them for their rejection of His sovereign rule by giving them exactly what they wanted.

After their first king, Saul, overstepped his bounds by usurping the prerogatives of a priest, God raised up David, a man after His own heart. David was the son of Jesse, in the line of Judah, through whom the Redeemer would come. As a man of war, David was not permitted to fulfill his heart's desire—building the temple of God. That honor went to the wisest man who ever lived, David's son, Solomon. Solomon built the temple, restored the ark of the covenant to the holy place, and reminded God of His promises to His people. Fire from heaven devoured the burnt offering on the altar, and the Shekinah glory filled the temple. But Solomon sinned by marrying foreign women who turned his heart away from God. After his death, dissension split the nation.

The southern kingdom retained the tribes of Judah and Benjamin and the capital city of Jerusalem, while the remaining tribes settled in the north around their capital of Samaria. The northern kingdom disintegrated quickly under idolatrous kings and fell to Syria in 722 B.C. The southern kingdom eventually followed suit, finally collapsing in 586 B.C. to Nebuchadnezzar's persistent assaults.

The exiles resisted full assimilation into the cultures of their foreign captors by establishing synagogues to preserve their worship and electing scribes to preserve their Scriptures. After Cyrus conquered Babylon in 539 B.C., he permitted the Jews to return to Jerusalem and rebuild their temple. A "remnant" returned to the land under Ezra and Nehemiah to rebuild the temple and the walls of Jerusalem, where they listened to Malachi proclaim the last prophecy they would hear for four hundred years.

At long last, God's silence was broken by the voice of an eccentric desert ascetic heralding the Redeemer and calling the people to repent. One seemingly unremarkable day, the Redeemer walked quietly out of the obscure environs of Galilee and submitted to the prophet's baptism before disappearing into the wilderness to prepare for His own mission.

He traversed the tiny nation, declaring Himself the expected Redeemer and substantiating His claims with miraculous powers. His ministry enraged the religious establishment and brought hope to the elect of every nation. His confrontational life precipitated His preordained death. He was executed on a cruel Roman cross, but could not be held by a sealed tomb. His followers claimed they had seen Him alive and attributed their boldness to the indwelling power of His Spirit. They glorified Him by declaring His truth in His "body," the church, and in completed Scripture, the New Testament writings.

Jesus Christ is one of a kind—the only man who was ever God; the only man who obeyed God's law; the only man who bore God's wrath against our sin; the only man who conquered death; the only man who opened heaven's door.

Christmas is all about Him: not only His birth but also His crucifixion—and His resurrection. It's about His being God, and why He lived, and died, and rose again. It's about our hopeless sin, and His unique propitiation, and God's gracious forgiveness. It's about a life like no other—God with us—the subject of our study.

Are you ready? Let's begin.

Primary Passages

John 1:1–18

Matthew 1–2

Luke 1:1–4; 1:26–2:52;
  3:23–38

Supplementary Passages

Hebrews 1–2

Philippians 2:5–11

Colossians 1:15–20; 2:8–12

Titus 2:11–14

Isaiah 7:14; 9:6–7; 52:13–53:12

Micah 5:2

Hosea 11:1

Jeremiah 31:15

Before reading the lesson material, please read the primary Scripture passages listed above and as many of the supplementary passages as time allows. Then briefly summarize in your notebook what you have read. (Do not go into detail. Limit your summary to whom the passages discuss, what is being discussed, and where and when the events in the passages occur.)

1

Immanuel,
God with Us

A girl on the brink of womanhood,
and the man who planned to marry her.
A frazzled innkeeper, and a frightened king.
A handful of poor shepherds,
and a band of wealthy travelers.
A godly old man, a saintly old widow,
and a group of astonished temple teachers.
An odd assortment of people these—
the first to encounter
Immanuel, God with us.

Benjamin Warfield captured the essence of the Gospels when he
said that they portray a human episode in the divine life.[1] They
are not, he says, formal biographies of a merely human life, but
biographical arguments written to emphasize different aspects of
that unique divine episode.

Warfield emphasized that the biographical arguments of the
Gospels are historically accurate as well as historically selective,
giving us four understandably different but completely reliable
accounts of the life of our Lord. Each writer chose from the store
of true biographical incidents those which would enhance his own
particular portrait.

Writing with Purpose
(Matthew 1:1–17; Luke 1:1–4; 3:23–28; John 1:1–18)

Matthew, Mark, Luke, and John each portray Jesus Christ from a distinct perspective. Matthew presents Him as the Jewish Messiah—the Prophet, Priest, and King promised in the Old Testament. Mark presents Him as a servant, who came not to be served but to serve and to give His life a ransom for many. Luke focuses on the humanity of Jesus, while John focuses on His deity.

The events found in each gospel support each writer's "argument." Matthew's gospel teems with Old Testament references highlighting the glorious fulfillment of messianic prophecies, while Mark's moves quickly from scene to scene depicting a busy servant. Luke documents the providential ordering of world events that worked out God's plan of redemption, and John highlights Jesus' display of His incarnate deity.

Even the genealogies enhance their author's perspectives.[2] Matthew's traces the kingly line of Joseph, substantiating Jesus' right to rule the nation of Israel. Mark's lack of a formal genealogy fits his picture of a servant. Luke traces Jesus' human ancestry through Mary's line, detailing the way God protected His Son's royal privilege by circumventing the cursed line of Jeconiah, from whom Joseph descended. And John's first eighteen verses contain a truly divine genealogy that establishes Jesus' oneness with God, His distinct personhood, and His perfect fulfillment of God's eternal decree.

As we embark on our brief study of the life of Christ, be aware that we cannot fully investigate all four gospel portraits of Jesus Christ. Rather, we will seek to develop a broad understanding of this life like no other that will lay a solid foundation for further study.

Surprising News for Mary
(Matthew 1:18–25; Luke 1:26–56)

We begin in Nazareth where a young, righteous Galilean virgin named Mary had just received an astounding message from the angel Gabriel. "Hail, favored one! The Lord is with you" (Luke 1:28). These long-anticipated words emphasized God's extension of grace to Mary, and her humble response reveals her understanding of its magnitude. "How can this be?" she marveled (v. 34) and submitted in faith to the angel's explanation.

The practical implications of her submissiveness were overwhelming. She was engaged to be married, still a virgin, and pregnant with the Messiah. Would anyone believe her? Could she believe it herself? To whom could she turn for faith-confirming encouragement? God's grace met all of these needs by directing the young girl to her cousin, Elizabeth, who had also miraculously conceived a child.

As Mary traveled, she must have wondered how to break her news, but upon arrival, she realized there was no need to do so. The moment Elizabeth saw her, she knew. Her child leaped in her womb, and she greeted Mary as the mother of her Messiah: "Blessed among women are you, and blessed is the fruit of your womb!" (v. 42). Mary responded with a beautiful song of praise and adoration that has become known in the church as the "Magnificat."

For three months the women shared the glorious blessing of shared participation in God's astonishing fulfillment of His covenant of redemption. The days passed quickly, and as Elizabeth's time drew near, Mary returned to Nazareth to face her betrothed husband.

It must have taken all of her courage to tell him her story and all of her faith to trust God with his doubts. But Joseph's divine appointment as the earthly provider and protector of Mary and her child assured his righteous response to her unsettling news. The couple's hasty marriage and the soon-to-be-obvious necessity of it may have fanned the flames of village gossip and made their mandatory trip to Bethlehem much less of a burden.

Not Just Another Christmas Story
(Matthew 2:1; Luke 2:1–7)
Luke's account of Jesus' birth has become something of a Christmas classic, cherished along with Charles Dickens's *A Christmas Carol* and Frank Capra's *It's a Wonderful Life*. However, its significance places it far above any other Christmas story.

Unlike Dickens and Capra, Luke intended not to "inspire" his readers to good will and brotherhood, but to describe God's intervention in human history to fulfill His covenant promises. Luke's simple story illustrates the profound theological mystery of the Incarnation.

The baby born in that Bethlehem manger was like no other. He was God in the flesh, born of a woman by the act of God. He was fully human, yet without sin; and He was fully God, yet subject to certain limitations. His advent had been perfectly planned before the world began and perfectly orchestrated throughout the ages.

God acted in history to accomplish His plan by ordaining certain pagan activities. A Roman census brought Joseph and Mary to Bethlehem just as "the days were completed for her to give birth" (v. 6). But scarce accommodations forced them into the shelter of a stable, where Mary delivered her firstborn son alone and unheralded.

Was this God's plan for the advent of the Messiah? Of course it was. But it certainly didn't square with Jewish expectations. The nation was looking for a deliverer from Rome, not a deliverer from sin. Few Jews recognized Him, and those who did seemed taken by surprise. His own godly mother lacked full understanding and pondered in her heart many mysteries about her son.

God was at work in the world—Immanuel, God with us. He was accomplishing His purposes through human agency but not under human control. The key participants could do little more than watch and wonder as He configured their circumstances to bring about His will.

Angels and Shepherds
(Luke 2:8–20)

Shepherds were not highly regarded in Jewish society. No Jew in his right mind would have expected God to disclose the momentous news of the Messiah's birth to such a lowly bunch. But God's ways are not our ways and His thoughts are not our thoughts. His unusual announcement, delivered by a host of angels, declared for all time that redemption was not limited to the strong, the powerful, the rich, the culturally elite, or even the Jews.

The angels brought "good news of a great joy *which shall be for all the people*" (v. 10).

The shepherds had no trouble getting the message—they knew the Messiah had come, and they knew where to find Him. Acting in faith, they went to Him, believed on Him, joyously told others about Him, and returned to their sheep "glorifying and praising God for all that they had heard and seen" (v. 20).

The message of the angels was full of theological significance regarding the identity of the Messiah. He was called a "Savior, who is Christ the Lord" (v. 11). His lordship is inexorably linked to His mission (Christ) and His work (Savior). In other words, Christ could not have been our Savior had He not been our Lord.

His coming brought "glory to God in the highest, and on earth peace among men with whom He is pleased" (v. 14). The human episode in the divine life reflected God's glory and secured salvation's peace for the elect.

Simeon and Anna
(Luke 2:21–39)

Joseph and Mary took no liberties with the child Messiah but faithfully fulfilled God's covenant requirements. On His eighth day of life they presented Him at the temple for circumcision and official declaration of His God-given name. His presentation and His mother's purification required a sacrificial offering, and the young family presented two turtledoves—the offering of the poor. Obviously, His messianic mission would not depend upon worldly advantages.

The family encountered two remarkable people in the temple. Simeon was a righteous old man, devoted to God, who prayed for the blessing of seeing the Lord's Messiah. When he took Jesus in his arms, he knew his prayer had been answered. His joyful prophecy, identifying the child as "a light for revelation to the Gentiles and the glory of Thy people Israel" (v. 32) reiterated the worldwide scope of His messianic mission. Anna, a devout widow who apparently lived and ministered full time in the temple, also recognized Jesus as the Messiah and proclaimed Him as Israel's Redeemer.

Simeon and Anna were true worshipers of God who were blessed for their faithfulness. As we proceed through our study, we will see a great contrast between the humble worship of people like them and the arrogant hypocrisy of most of their leaders.

Visitors from the East
(Matthew 2:1–23)

Matthew, supporting his distinct biographical argument, is the only gospel writer to record the visit of the Magi, whose arrival fulfilled the prophecy of Micah 5:1–2 and whose departure unleashed the holocaust described in Jeremiah 31:15.

The wise men (Magi) were probably pagan astrologers familiar with the Hebrew Scriptures. Their study of the heavens in connection with Jewish prophecy alerted them to the significance of an unusual phenomenon occurring around the time of Jesus' birth. Perhaps convinced that the Jewish Messiah had been born, they set out to find Him.

What was it they saw? A supernatural occurrence, or a natural phenomenon? We have no way of knowing, and it really doesn't matter. God could have used either to draw them to Bethlehem.

The wise men, expecting the Jewish leaders to know about the birth, went to Jerusalem and asked for directions. Their surprise at Herod's ignorance of the matter was obviously equaled by Herod's alarm at their questions. He lived in fear of the volatile mix of political unrest and messianic expectations in his kingdom that threatened to blast him off the throne at the slightest provocation. This child could provoke just such a fiasco and would have to be eliminated immediately.

Knowing he could not fool his fellow Jews with devout pretensions, he secretly directed his foreign visitors to proceed to Bethlehem, find the child, and return to tell him where he could also go and worship Him. They located the child but never returned to Herod. God warned them in a dream to go home without facilitating Herod's diabolical plan.

When Herod realized the eastern visitors weren't coming back, his raging paranoia unleashed a blood bath in Bethlehem. Words can't convey the anguish of parents who stood in the wake of his madness, but not even such wickedness could thwart God's plan. The angel warned Joseph to flee with his family to the safety of Egypt and to remain in that country until called to return.

Childhood
(Luke 2:40–52)

If the Incarnation staggers your imagination as much as it does mine, the idea of God incarnate living out a "normal" childhood in a small Galilean village will boggle your mind. Yet Jesus apparently did just that. He was the eldest son in a large family (Mark 6:3), attended school, helped His father in the family business, and played with other children. As He grew, He also participated in the Jewish rituals of manhood and by the age of twelve, was traveling with His parents to Jerusalem to observe the Passover.

Following His first such observance, His parents departed for home with friends while He remained in the temple, astounding the teachers with His understanding of God's truth. Joseph and Mary finally missed Him, frantically tracked Him to the temple, and hastily reprimanded Him for His seeming inconsideration, only to be reminded of who He was: "Did you not know that I had to be in My Father's house?" (Luke 2:49).

Luke summarizes the next eighteen years of His life in one masterfully brief but comprehensive sentence: "And Jesus kept increasing in wisdom and stature and in favor with God and men" (v. 52). Even though Luke gives us no details, he clearly communicates that Jesus matured mentally, physically, spiritually, and socially as only He could. He became the perfect human being, suited in every way to fulfill God's glorious purpose for the human episode in the divine life.

Notes

1. Space does not permit a full treatment of the great doctrines associated with the life of Christ. Students unfamiliar with these doctrines are encouraged to pursue further study and

will find B. B. Warfield's *Person and Work of Christ* and R. C. Sproul's *The Glory of Christ* invaluable resources.

2. For a detailed analysis of these genealogies, see William Hendriksen's commentaries on Matthew and Luke.

Exercises

Review

1. On the blank map in appendix C, locate and mark Jerusalem, Bethlehem, Nazareth, and Egypt. Also locate the regions of Galilee, Judea, and Samaria, and shade them in with different colored pencils.

2. Describe each gospel writer's purpose for writing, and give some examples of how each man accomplished his purpose. How does understanding these purposes for writing explain the apparent inconsistencies in the four gospel records?

3. Apply Isaiah 55:8–9 to the major events surrounding Jesus' birth.

4. Reread Matthew 1:18–25 and Luke 1:26–56. Describe, in your own words, Joseph and Mary's reactions to the words of the angel; emphasize how their reactions reflect their individual heart attitudes toward God. Be as creative as you like—try your hand at a poem, a song, or a story—but don't allow your creativity to abuse the scriptural account.

5. Reread Luke 2:8–39 and Matthew 2:1–12. Compare and contrast the reactions of the shepherds, Simeon, Anna, the wise men, and Herod to the birth of the Christ child. Explain your understanding of why God included the reactions of these particular people to His Son in His inspired revelation. Support your understanding with Scripture if you can.

6. Explain how the angels' description of the baby as "a Savior, who is Christ the Lord" (Luke 2:11) reflects His mission and His work.

7. Explain the significance of Luke's all-encompassing summary of Jesus' childhood, "And Jesus kept increasing in wisdom and stature and in favor with God and men" (v. 52).

Application

1. In light of your answers to review exercises 4 and 5, describe how the reactions of these people to the birth of Christ should affect the ways you will or will not celebrate Christmas this year.

   Joseph and Mary:
   the shepherds:
   Simeon and/or Anna:
   the wise men:
   Herod:

Digging Deeper

1. James Montgomery Boice, in his commentary on Philippians, describes Philippians 2:5–11 as the "Great Parabola of Scripture": the passage begins with Christ's equality with God in heaven, descends with Him to His humiliation on earth, and then ascends again to reveal His exaltation to the right hand of God. Read these verses carefully with Boice's description in mind, and compare them to John's "divine genealogy" of Jesus Christ in John 1:1–18. Describe the similarities you see between these two passages, and explain the significance of these similarities.

2. Many of the great doctrines of the church were formulated from biblical principles in response to heresy. For example, the enduring statement of the foundational doctrine of the Trinity was formulated at the Council of Nicaea in A.D. 325 in response to the heresy of Monarchianism or Sabellianism. The key statement of Christ's two natures came out of the Council of Chalcedon in A.D. 451 in response to the heresies of Arianism and Docetism.

Study the historical events that necessitated the formulation of these particular doctrinal statements and the biblical passages relevant to them. Then explain why an accurate biblical understanding of both the Trinity and the two natures of Christ is essential to an accurate biblical understanding of salvation.

Primary Passages

Luke 1:5–25; 57–80; 3:1–20
John 1:19–36
Matthew 3:13–4:11

Supplementary Passages

Mark 1:1–11
Matthew 3:1–12
Luke 3:21–22; 4:1–13

Before reading the lesson material, please read the primary Scripture passages listed above and as many of the supplementary passages as time allows. Then briefly summarize in your notebook what you have read. (Do not go into detail. Limit your summary to whom the passages discuss, what is being discussed, and where and when the events in the passages occur.)

2

Behold the Lamb of God

John the Baptist and Jesus of Nazareth.
The one, the herald; the other, the Heralded.
What a day it was when they met in the
wilderness to inaugurate God's plan.
The herald proclaimed Messiah's arrival with
words comprehensible to all who could hear.
"Behold, the Lamb of God!"

There are a dozen Ruvolos listed in the Albuquerque telephone book, and all of them are related—to my husband. Like most large Italian families, we enjoy getting together, and every time we do, I marvel at the diversity among us. If I didn't *know* we were all related, I wouldn't believe it!

The people living in first-century Israel may have been equally amazed to discover that Jesus, the responsible young man from Nazareth, and John, the eccentric desert prophet, were cousins. Even though the circumstances of their births were equally unusual, they had little else in common.

Jesus grew to manhood in the quiet confines of a large Galilean family, while John matured in a rugged expanse of Judean wilderness, orphaned and alone. Jesus dressed, worked, and socialized as a typical Jewish man and fit in with His culture. John, however, with his wild appearance and rugged lifestyle, lived on the fringes of society. But as different as they were, both played essential roles in God's unfolding plan of redemption.

The Birth of John
(Luke 1:5–25, 57–80)

As Luke's gospel opens, the Jews had not heard from their God for four hundred years. Had He forgotten them? Abandoned them? No. His silence was purposeful—an essential element in His plan. It was the silence of breathless anticipation—the culmination of an eternity of preparation. The orchestra of heaven sat motionless, poised over their celestial instruments, eyes fixed on the uplifted arms of the Divine Conductor, waiting for His cue.

The time had come to announce the Messiah. The herald's name would be John. People would call him "the Baptist." He would be born miraculously and live distinctively. His prophetic voice would break God's long silence by calling the people to repent—for the kingdom of heaven was at hand.

His parents, Zechariah and Elizabeth, were humble, righteous Jews of Levitical lineage who served God faithfully even as they bore the humiliating stigma of childlessness in a culture that disdained the barren. Their earnest prayers for a child had dwindled and died with advancing age, but their equally earnest prayers for Israel's deliverance by the promised Messiah grew stronger every day.

Zechariah loved serving in the temple and cherished the hope of receiving the once-in-a-lifetime privilege of offering the incense in the Holy Place. What joy he felt the day the lot fell to him! And how unprepared he was for what followed!

The unexpected appearance of God's angelic messenger Gabriel delivering God's answer to Zechariah's prayers completely overwhelmed the righteous old priest. He and Elizabeth would have a son—a son who would prepare the way for the Messiah! The simultaneous granting of his most ardent prayers on this day of all days stretched his faith thin and flooded his soul with doubt. Instead of gratefully acknowledging God's graciousness to him, he questioned the angel and asked for a sign.

And a sign he received—apropos to his doubt. The old priest was struck dumb until the birth of his son. Then, when he confirmed Elizabeth's insistence upon the child's unprecedented name, his speech was restored. Just as doubt had tied his tongue, faith had freed it, unleashing the pent-up praises of his heart. His prophetic hymn, recorded in Luke 1:68–79 and known in the church as the "Benedictus," praises God for the glorious fulfillment of His purposes.

The Ministry of John
(Matthew 3:1–12; Mark 1:1–8; Luke 3:1–20; John 1:19–36)

Luke summarizes John the Baptist's youth much as he does that of our Lord—in one thought-provoking sentence: "And the child continued to grow, and to become strong in spirit, and he lived in the deserts until the day of his public appearance to Israel" (1:80). As rich in concept as it is meager in detail, it allows some cautious speculation about John's childhood.

His strength of spirit may have come, in part, from the persistent instruction of elderly parents who knew their time with him would be short. They almost certainly invested those precious hours recounting the angelic prophecies surrounding his birth and teaching him the ancient Hebrew Scriptures he would participate in fulfilling.

John probably took up residence in the desert when his parents died. There he lived off the land, dressing in camel's hair and leather while subsisting on locust and wild honey. His strange lifestyle and unusual appearance may have convinced some that he was crazy and others that he was Elijah returned from the dead.

John's message, although far from pleasant, drew large crowds from near and far. He demanded repentance because the kingdom of heaven was at hand, and adapted the common practice of "washings"[1] into a baptism of repentance signifying confession of sin and commitment to righteousness. His teaching scandalized many self-righteous Jews who understood the symbolic cleansing ritual as appropriate for "filthy Gentiles" but hardly necessary for God's chosen people. John challenged their prideful beliefs by confronting them with their own uncleanness.

He refused to tolerate hypocritical seekers, vilifying the Pharisees and Sadducees as a "brood of vipers," disparaging their motives in coming to him, and demanding that they "bring forth fruit in keeping with repentance" (Luke 3:7–8). He belittled their standard defensive appeal to their Abrahamic lineage by reminding them that God could raise up children of Abraham out of the rocks and stones lying on the ground around them.

Honest seekers were given honest answers. Those with sufficient food and clothing were instructed to share. Publicans were told to collect no more than their due. Soldiers were admonished to refrain from violence, make no unwarranted accusations, and be content with their wages.

John's message of repentance was not an end in itself. He declared his work preparatory for that of the One who was coming after him, the One whose shoes he was not worthy to untie, the One who would baptize with the Holy Ghost and with fire. Using the powerful illustration of a winnowing fan separating wheat from chaff, John described how this One would gather His chosen ones to Himself and cast the remainder into unquenchable fire.

John's impact on the people of Israel greatly concerned their leaders, who sent an official delegation to Bethany to question him about his identity. Their questions may have reflected the speculative gossip running rampant through the populace. However, John steadfastly denied being the Messiah, Elijah, or "the prophet" of Deuteronomy 18:15. He identified himself only as "the voice of one crying in the wilderness," who would prepare the way for the coming of the Lord (John 1:23).

The Baptism of Jesus
(Matthew 3:13–17; Mark 1:9–11; Luke 3:21–22)

The moment when John looked up and saw Jesus standing quietly among those waiting for baptism must have electric. Scripture doesn't tell us whether the two men had ever met, but it does tell us that John recognized His Messiah immediately. He admonished the crowd to "behold, the Lamb of God who takes away the sins of the world" (John 1:29) and then adamantly declared, "He must increase, but I must decrease" (John 3:30).

John was shocked when Jesus, the Lamb without blemish, asked for baptism. But Jesus insisted, "Permit it at this time; for in this way it is fitting for us to fulfill all righteousness" (Matthew 3:15).

What did He mean by fulfilling all righteousness? Simply that His baptism was a necessary part of His mission of reconciliation. He had to *identify* with fallen men and women in their sinfulness—although He had no sinfulness of His own—so that they could be *identified* with Him in His righteousness—although they had no righteousness of their own. His baptism signified His identification with those He came to save—an identification that would be fulfilled (or completed) on the cross.[2]

Jesus' baptism declared His deep love for His own and generated approval from the voice of His Father as the Spirit descended in the form of a dove to visibly strengthen the Son for His task.

In recording this momentous event, Luke has given us one of Scripture's clearest defenses of the reality of the Trinity. All three members of the Godhead appeared *together* to inaugurate Their plan of redemption. The triune God is pictured as one essence (united in purpose and mission) but as three distinct persons—the Son in submission to the Father's will in the power of the Holy Spirit, the Father declaring His pleasure in the Son's action through the Holy Spirit, and the Holy Spirit descending from the Father to rest upon the Son.

The Temptation of Jesus
(Matthew 4:1–11; Mark 1:12–13; Luke 4:1–13)

Immediately following Jesus' baptism, the Spirit drove Him into the solitude of the wilderness to prepare for His mission. For forty days, He would forego physical nourishment and rely solely on spiritual sustenance as He fought off Satan's attacks. The temptation of Jesus, although uniquely His own, teaches us much about fighting ours, too. Satan's key to temptation is his plan of attack. He knew that Jesus, although weak and tired, was fully committed to His ministry. Therefore, Satan did not attempt to dissuade Jesus from His mission. Instead, he offered him a "better way" to get the job done.

First, he appealed to Jesus' ability to meet physical needs. Why not satisfy His hunger by using His miraculous powers to turn the inexhaustible supply of desert stones into bread? Since He had created them in the first place, why not recreate them now? Jesus responded, "It is written, 'Man shall not live on bread alone, but on every word that proceeds out of the mouth of God' " (Matthew 4:4). By drawing on the spiritual resources available in God's Word, He lived out what He would later teach His disciples, "Seek first His kingdom and His righteousness; and all these things shall be added to you" (Matthew 6:33).

Satan, however, wasn't finished. He had two more attack plans, which Matthew and Luke reverse in presenting—most likely to support their individual biographical arguments. Both writers seem to present the temptations in order of their readers' perception of their intensity. The Jews addressed by Matthew would regard improper worship the greater temptation, while the Gentiles addressed by Luke would bestow that honor upon loss of life.

Following Matthew's account, we find Satan taking Jesus to the "pinnacle of the temple"—possibly the edge of the roof of Herod's royal portico. Looking down from there 450 feet to the floor of the Kidron Valley, Satan said, in effect, "God has promised to protect you, right? So, go ahead and jump. What better way to launch your ministry than with a dramatic demonstration of God's endorsement right here in the heart of Jerusalem?" (Matthew 4:6, my paraphrase). Jesus again responded with Scripture: "You shall not put the LORD your God to the test" (v. 7).

Two plans had been foiled, but the last was ingenious—a guaranteed shortcut to world dominion. Taking Jesus to the top of a high mountain, Satan offered Him all the kingdoms of the world in return for His worship. Jesus' reply was decisive: "Begone, Satan! For it is written, 'You shall worship the LORD your God and serve Him only' " (v. 10). Satan knew he was beaten, at least for the moment. He withdrew "until an opportune time" (Luke 4:13), and angels arrived to minister to Jesus.

Jesus' temptation in the wilderness alerts us to one of Satan's most successful ploys: encouraging us to pursue God's work with worldly methods. And he is not above wrenching Scripture out of context to do it. Jesus' ability to handle accurately the Word of

God enabled Him to recognize deception and ward off temptation. We do well to learn from His example.

Notes

1. These washings were performed in purification rites and during the initiations of Jewish proselytes.

2. The theological term associated with this identification process is *imputation*.

Exercises

Review

1. William Hendriksen describes "the wilderness" where John preached as the rolling badlands between the hill country of Judea in the west and the Dead Sea and lower Jordan in the east and extending north to where the Jabbok flows into the Jordan. Locate and mark this area on the map in appendix C. Donald Guthrie indicates that the location of Jesus' temptation was the lonely region of desert in the region of Judea just east of Bethlehem. Locate and mark this area on the map in appendix C also. Note the distance Jesus traveled from Nazareth to meet John in the wilderness.

2. Reread Luke 1:5–25 and 57–80, and describe the miraculous nature of John's birth. Do you see a connection between the circumstances of John's birth and the mission to which he was called? If so, explain.

3. Describe the similarities and differences between the angelic visitations received by Mary and Zechariah, including their responses. How can you benefit from the example of these two people?

4. Reread Matthew 3:1–12, Mark 1:1–8, Luke 3:1–20, and John 1:19–36, and summarize John's message to the people of his

day. Why did he call them specifically to repent? Why was his message harder for Jews to accept than it was for Gentiles?

5. Explain the reason Jesus gave John regarding the necessity of His baptism.

6. Reread Matthew 4:1-11, Mark 1:12-13, and Luke 4:1-13, and describe the temptations Jesus faced in the wilderness. How did He respond to these temptations? How can you benefit from His example?

Application

1. Read 1 John 2:15-17 and relate John's teaching to the temptations Jesus faced in the wilderness. Now read Genesis 3:1-7 and relate the 1 John passage and the Gospel accounts of Jesus' temptation to the temptation of Adam and Eve in the Garden of Eden. (Concentrate on the similarities between the temptations of Adam and Eve and Jesus, and on their responses.)

    List specific examples of how you have been tempted and how you responded to temptation in each of these areas:

    the lust of the flesh:
    the lust of the eyes:
    the boastful pride of life:

    Now, study Hebrews 4:14-16 and describe the hope you find in these verses.

Digging Deeper

1. Scholars disagree about whether it was possible for Jesus to sin. Some, such as Charles Hodge, believe that if Jesus could not sin, the temptations He endured reduce to a mere sham. He states, "Temptation implies the possibility of sin. If from the constitution of his person, it was impossible for Christ to sin, then his temptation was unreal and without effect, and

He cannot sympathize with His people" (Charles Hodge, *Systematic Theology* 3 vols. [Grand Rapids: Eerdmans, reprinted 1993], 2:457).

Other scholars, such as John Walvoord, believe that Jesus' unique union of two natures makes it possible and necessary that He be temptable (in His human nature) yet unable to sin (in His divine nature). Walvoord states, "The idea that temptability implies susceptibility is unsound. While the temptation may be real, there may be infinite power to resist that temptation and if this power is infinite, the person is impeccable [unable to sin]." Walvoord elaborates by citing William G. T. Shedd's statement that just because an army cannot be defeated does not mean it cannot be attacked (John Walvoord, *Jesus Christ Our Lord* [Chicago: Moody Press, 1969], 147).

Research this issue and summarize the arguments of the major proponents of each view. Which view do you believe coincides most clearly with what Scripture teaches about Jesus Christ? Support your answer with Scripture references.

Primary Passages
Luke 4:14–30
John 2–4

Supplementary Passages
Matthew 4:12–17
Mark 1:14–15
Isaiah 9:1–2

Before reading the lesson material, please read the primary Scripture passages listed above and as many of the supplementary passages as time allows. Then briefly summarize in your notebook what you have read. (Do not go into detail. Limit your summary to whom the passages discuss, what is being discussed, and where and when the events in the passages occur.)

3

The Kingdom of Heaven Is at Hand

Mary realized it at a wedding.
A sordid assembly of religious
opportunists faced it in the temple.
A proud Pharisee learned it at night.
And a disgraced woman grasped it by a well.
John had to explain it to His disciples.
But the folks in Nazareth refused to believe it.
What did they see as they brushed shoulders with Jesus?
A startling reality they could not simply ignore:
The kingdom of heaven is at hand.

Members of England's Flat Earth Society, as their name implies, deny that the earth is round. Christopher Columbus, they say, was deluded. Astronauts only *think* they are circling the earth. In reality, they are traveling in ellipses parallel to the earth. And ships appearing to dip below the horizon do not testify to the curvature of the earth, but only to a quirky trick of perspective.

Most of us snicker at such "silly" ideas without pausing to consider how resistant we too can be to *changing our minds.* We hate to admit we are wrong. We choke on the words, "You are right." We avoid controversial issues and refuse to listen to those who challenge our cherished beliefs. Our minds are made up, and we don't want to be confused with the facts—thank you very much!

Perhaps that's why straightforward presentations of the gospel are so offensive to unbelievers. The gospel demands that we change our minds—and we don't want to do that. The gospel demands that we stop thinking of ourselves as "pretty good people" and start thinking of ourselves as desperately depraved sinners. It demands that we stop thinking about God as the benevolent, kindly "man upstairs" and start thinking of Him as a wrathful, righteous Judge. It demands that we stop thinking about our ability to take care of ourselves and start thinking about our complete dependence on Someone Else.

As Jesus began His ministry, He challenged people to change their minds—about themselves, about God, and about Him. None of them found His challenge easy, but all responded, either righteously or sinfully. And the way they responded determined their eternal destiny.

A Wedding at Cana
(John 2:1–11)

One of the very first people Jesus challenged was His own mother. They were attending a wedding in the village of Cana, not far from Nazareth. When the wine ran out before the festivities were over, Mary took the socially embarrassing situation to her son, obviously expecting Him to do something about it. Scripture doesn't tell us what her motives were, but most of the commentators are eager to speculate. Some suggest she had been widowed at an early age and naturally looked to Jesus as the head of her household, while others read into her action a motherly push to get on with His messianic work.

Even though we can't be sure what Mary was thinking, we can safely assume that Jesus' response challenged her thinking. In two short sentences, He completely redefined their relationship. The Man who had accompanied her to the wedding as her son would escort her home as her Lord.

His words sound harsh to our modern ears, but in that day and time would not have seemed so. The term "woman," a respectful form of address in their culture, would be used again by Jesus at the hour of His death when He commended Mary into the care of His beloved disciple, John.

Jesus' remaining words constitute a firm but tender announcement of His final departure from her home. "What do I have to do with you? My hour has not yet come" (v. 4). God's will demanded that He now broaden His focus from submission to her wishes to His reason for being.

I sometimes wonder if the sword of Simeon's thirty-year-old prophecy began its relentless piercing of Mary's heart at that very moment. She turned from her son and said to the servants, "Whatever He says to you, do it" (v. 5). She had responded well to His challenge and changed her mind. She would no longer think of Him primarily as her son, but as the Son of God, her Lord and her Savior.

Jesus then acted, in accordance with the will of God, to transform well over a hundred gallons of water into excellent wine. His action blessed the wedding celebrants with joy, manifested His glory as the Son of God, and stimulated His disciples' belief in Him—thus laying a sound precedent of purpose for all the miracles that would follow.

Cleaning Out the Temple
(John 2:12–22)

The wedding at Cana marked a difficult time of transition for Mary. Her relationship with her first-born son had been irrevocably altered, and her life would never be the same. Jesus' love for her motivated Him to accompany His family to Capernaum where He helped them settle in before departing to celebrate the Passover in Jerusalem.

Upon entering the temple, Jesus was struck by the blasphemous incongruity between the scene before Him and the true meaning of Passover. Greedy temple officials were busily taking mercenary advantage of God's ritual sacrifices without giving a thought to the gracious atonement they pictured.

As Jesus watched, His righteous wrath escalated and eventually erupted in an explosive challenge to their hypocritical thinking. The temple officials scattered in panic before Jesus' whip, then regrouped to pompously question His authority to act. His answer, "Destroy this temple, and in three days I will raise it up" (v. 19), described His own ultimate fulfillment of the sacrificial rites. Tragically, however, it bounced right off their firmly made-up minds and failed to alter their hell-bent course.

"Nick at Night"
(John 2:23–3:21)

The signs Jesus performed in Jerusalem at Passover drew a curious crowd of shallow thrill-seekers whose "belief in His name" revolved around little more than His ability to perform miracles. From the midst of this untrustworthy crowd, however, one cautious Pharisee emerged as something of an anomaly. He was willing to learn, but hesitant to commit himself.

Nicodemus came to Jesus at night, filled with questions and fearful of what his colleagues would think if they knew he had come. Jesus didn't wait for the nervous Pharisee to voice his questions before challenging his traditional commitment to works righteousness.

"Truly, truly, I say to you, unless one is born again, he cannot see the kingdom of God" (John 3:3). Entering the kingdom of God requires one to be born "of water and the Spirit" because "that which is born of the flesh is flesh, and that which is born of the Spirit is spirit" (vv. 5–6).

Nicodemus was baffled. "How can these things be?" he protested (v. 9). Jesus elaborated with a helpful Old Testament analogy. Comparing Himself to the serpent lifted up in the wilderness, He drove home the point that just as those who looked to the serpent in obedience were healed physically, those who looked to Him in faith would be healed spiritually.

He then proceeded to describe God's incomparable love that compelled Him to send His Son to atone for man's sin. The Son who had come as the "light of the world" would either draw men to Himself or drive them further into the darkness. Would the "righteous" Pharisee change his mind? Would he bow to God's absolute sovereignty and relinquish all thoughts of earning eternal life? John doesn't tell us here, but he gives us reason to think so later in his gospel (see John 19:39–40).

Competition with John the Baptist
(John 3:22–36)

As Jesus and His disciples moved into the land of Judea teaching, baptizing, and attracting followers, some of John's disciples approached their leader with grave concerns about the future of their ministry. Many of John's followers were now following Jesus. Shouldn't they do something to stop the defections?

John responded with a reminder of what he had already told them. He was *not* the Messiah; his entire purpose was to herald the Messiah, rejoice in His success, and decrease as He increased. John then summarized the mission of the Messiah and exhorted them to change their minds. "He who believes in the Son has eternal life; but he who does not obey the Son shall not see life, but the wrath of God abides on him" (v. 36).

Appointment at a Well
(John 4:1–42)

As Jesus' ascending ministry drew dangerous attention from the Pharisees, He wisely decided to withdraw to Galilee, taking the unconventional route directly though Samaria. Arriving in Sychar around noon, the weary Messiah dispatched His disciples to rustle up some lunch before settling Himself by the well to wait for His divine appointment.

It wasn't long before He spotted her—a solitary woman making her way cautiously toward the well, obviously surprised and a bit suspicious to see Him there. She rarely encountered anyone at the well. The respectable women of Sychar didn't associate with the likes of her, and their hypocritical husbands never sought her out until after dark.

As she drew nearer, her suspicions were confirmed. He was a Jew and wouldn't waste His breath speaking to a Samaritan woman. When He did speak, she was astonished. "How is it that You, being a Jew, ask me for a drink since I am a Samaritan woman?" she asked (v. 9), only to be more astonished by His answer.

This hot, dusty, tired Jewish traveler had something called "living water" that would eliminate thirst. That would eliminate her midday treks to the well, timed to avoid the scorn of the women who gathered there in the cool mornings and evenings. Her eyes brightened at the thought of a miraculous means of escaping this miserable consequence of her sinful lifestyle but quickly clouded when Jesus said to her, "Go, call your husband" (v. 16).

"I have no husband," she blurted (v. 17), only to find that He already knew—about her five husbands, and about the nonhusband with whom she was currently living. Unwilling to stand exposed in the glaring light of His unsettling knowledge, she deftly shifted the spotlight back onto Him.

"Sir, I perceive that You are a prophet," she began (v. 19), hoping to draw His attention away from her personal life by opening the centuries-old, racially charged debate over temple worship. Jesus graciously neglected to drag her back to the original issue, but capitalized on her evasive maneuver by challenging her prejudicially conditioned mindset.

Affirming God's truth, that salvation is of the Jews, He informed her that true worship was not associated with a location but with the heart. "God is spirit, and those who worship Him must worship in spirit and truth" (v. 24). He then confronted her with the startling revelation that He Himself was the Messiah she had been taught to expect. The disciples picked this stunning moment to return, sending the discomforted woman scurrying back to town. She immediately reported to the men (perhaps a more receptive audience than the women) that she had met a man who knew all about her and wondered aloud if He might be the Christ.

Meanwhile back at the well, the disciples, completely oblivious to the drama that had just played out and confused by Jesus' refusal to eat, were facing a challenge of their own. Jesus, using the fields around them as an example, cautioned them against thinking that the "harvest" was still far in the future. All around them were Samaritan souls ready for harvest, and they must not neglect the opportunity because of prejudice.

No sooner were the words out of His mouth than the disciples looked to see that the road into town was indeed "white for harvest" (v. 35). A multitude of white-robed Samaritans had believed the woman's report and were streaming out to the well to hear more. The willingness of a Samaritan woman and the Jewish disciples to change their minds bore fruit two days later when the believing Samaritans told the woman, "It is no longer because of what you said that we believe, for we have heard for ourselves and know that this One is indeed the Savior of the world" (v. 42).

Galilee
(Matthew 4:12; Mark 1:14–15; Luke 4:14–15; John 4:43–54)

Jesus and His disciples were greeted in Galilee by many who had heard of His astonishing works at the Feast in Jerusalem and gathered expectantly in their synagogues to hear Him take up the message temporarily quelled by John's imprisonment: "The time is fulfilled, and the kingdom of God is at hand; repent and believe in the gospel" (Mark 1:15).

One distraught Galilean nobleman was particularly excited about Jesus' return. He lived in Cana and had heard about the miraculous provision of wine at a local wedding. His son now lay dying, and in fatherly desperation, he set out for Capernaum to find Jesus and beg Him to perform another miracle.

Jesus listened and offered this man a challenge similar to those He had extended to so many others. "Unless you people see signs and wonders, you simply will not believe" (John 4:48). Was the nobleman ready to change his mind about Jesus? Was he willing to stop thinking of Him as a sensational attraction and trust in His unadorned word of assurance? "Go your way," Jesus told the man. "Your son lives" (v. 50).

The nobleman lost no time getting back on the road to Cana. He had indeed been willing to change his mind about Jesus. He accepted His word without demand for drama—or even His presence. The emotional intensity of his encounter with Jesus must have peaked when he spotted a small band of his own servants traveling to meet him. Had his change of mind been warranted? Was his son alive or dead?

What joy to discover he was alive! And that he had been healed at the exact moment the Messiah had spoken. Just as he had wasted no time rushing to Jesus, he now wasted no time rushing to tell His story. The nobleman's change of mind had brought forth a saving faith that soon gave birth to a saved family. Everyone living in his house believed.

You Can't Go Home Again
(Matthew 4:13–17; Luke 4:16–30)

Jesus' final visit to Nazareth illustrates the adage "Familiarity breeds contempt." Having heard about His remarkable activities in Judea and Galilee, the leaders of His home synagogue seemed eager to hear Him when they offered Him the honor of teaching on the Sabbath. He chose for His topic the words of the prophet Isaiah, "The Spirit of the Lord is upon Me, because He anointed Me to preach the gospel to the poor. He has sent Me to proclaim release to the captives, and recovery of sight to the blind, to set free those who are downtrodden, to proclaim the favorable year of the Lord" (Luke 4:18–19).

But the mood of the hometown crowd soon changed when He sat down to teach. "Today this Scripture has been fulfilled in your hearing" (v. 21). His words were met with stunned silence. He was claiming to be their Messiah! The son of Joseph and Mary had become a blasphemer.

Jesus appealed to them to change their minds by reminding them of two Old Testament prophets whose ministries were scorned by their own people and benefited Gentiles instead. The people of Nazareth were too furious to listen, however, and attempted to stone Him to death. But Jesus, knowing His hour had not yet come, passed "through their midst" and "went His way" (v. 30).

From that point on, Capernaum was His home and the center of His ministry. Matthew sees the relocation as a fulfillment of the prophecy found in Isaiah 9:1–2.

> The land of Zebulun and the land of Naphtali,
> By the way of the sea, beyond the Jordan, Galilee of
>   the Gentiles—

> The people who were sitting in darkness saw a great
>   light,
> And to those who were sitting in the land and shadow
>   of death,
> Upon them a light dawned.
>   (Matthew 4:15–16)

The prophecy does indeed speak of the relocation, but it also speaks of much more. The light had dawned. The people no longer sat in darkness. And those who saw clearly enough to change their minds escaped the shadow of death.

Exercises

Review

1. On the map in appendix C, locate and mark the cities of Cana and Capernaum and the region of Samaria. See if you can determine the route most Jews would have taken when traveling between Judea and Galilee.

2. Describe how the gospel, properly presented, challenges unbelievers to change their minds.

3. Explain why Jesus challenged His mother to change her mind about Him *before* He performed the miracle at the wedding in Cana. How did that miracle lay a precedent for the miracles Jesus would perform in the future?

4. Compare and contrast the responses of Mary, the temple officials, Nicodemus, John's disciples, the Samaritan woman, the Galilean nobleman, and the people of Nazareth to Jesus. In your answer, consider the challenges Jesus presented to each, how each reacted to His challenge, and the outcome of each reaction.

5. Reread John 2–4 and describe how Jesus presented the truth about Himself (the gospel) to each of the people with whom

He came in contact. What can you learn about presenting the gospel to unbelievers from His example?

6. Explain the significance of the prophecy found in Isaiah 9:1–2.

Application

1. Think back to when you first heard the gospel. Did it challenge your thinking? If so, explain. How have you changed your thinking about yourself, about God, and about Jesus Christ since becoming a Christian? Spend some time in prayer asking God to reveal to you any other areas in which your thinking needs to change.

2. Pick one of the people Jesus challenged in this lesson, and describe in detail how his or her example has encouraged you to think correctly about yourself, about God, and/or about Jesus Christ.

3. Adapt one of the incidents in this lesson to use in teaching children or young people the importance of thinking correctly about themselves, about God, and/or about Jesus Christ. Be as creative as you can. Write a Bible story, a skit, a role play, or a game, and try to include activities that encourage participation and application.

Digging Deeper

1. Commentators disagree about the meaning of Jesus' reference to "water" in John 3:5. Some say this is a reference to physical birth, some think it refers to baptism, some connect it with Scripture, and a few indicate that it is another reference to the Spirit used solely for emphasis.

   Research this issue, being sure to study the arguments of at least one commentator who holds each of the above viewpoints. Which argument do you think is best supported by Scripture? How might your understanding of what Jesus means by His reference to water affect your understanding of the point He is making to Nicodemus? Explain your answer fully.

Primary Passages	Supplementary Passages
Mark 1:16–3:19	Matthew 4:18–25; 8:1–4,
Luke 4:31–6:16	14–17; 9:1–17; 12:1–21
Matthew 10:2–4	Acts 1:13, 15–26
	Isaiah 42:1–4

Before reading the lesson material, please read the primary Scripture passages listed above and as many of the supplementary passages as time allows. Then briefly summarize in your notebook what you have read. (Do not go into detail. Limit your summary to whom the passages discuss, what is being discussed, and where and when the events in the passages occur.)

4

New Wine

*Jesus Christ
disrupted religious traditions,
enraged religious legalists,
and changed common people.
A master revolutionary
bent on destroying God's law?
No, rather a master restorationist
bent on producing receptacles
fit to receive His
new wine.*

Many of the world's languages are marked by distinctive qualities that set them apart from all others. Spanish rolls off the tongue with graceful eloquence, French tingles with romance, the king's English marches resolutely past stiff upper lips, and German snaps with authority. Each language, because of its peculiar characteristics, seems uniquely suited for particular purposes. Passionate love letters should always be written in French; "The Via Dolorosa" should only be sung in Spanish; Shakespeare's plays always lose something in translation; and Hitler's speeches, in any other language, wouldn't have wielded such phenomenal power.

The language of the New Testament, koine Greek, is also

uniquely suited for a particular task—that of communicating God's eternal truths. Greek is an extremely precise language, capable of conveying subtle nuances of meaning that are frequently obscured in other languages.[1] For example, three different Greek words are translated into English as "love," two different Greek words are translated "another," two are frequently translated "patience," and two are translated "new."

Understanding the difference between the words translated "new," *kainos* and *neos,* gives us a key insight into the early ministry of Jesus Christ. *Kainos* is newness that is qualitatively different from what has been before, while *neos* is newness with respect to time and is used of something newly come into being or become present.[2]

Jesus' ministry disrupted the Jewish status quo because it was *neos,* not *kainos.* He had recently (newly) arrived on the scene proclaiming a message that, although not qualitatively different from anything God had said before, certainly sounded that way. God's people has so distorted God's truth with human tradition that they no longer recognized its purest form.

Before they could receive the *neos* truth Jesus brought them, they themselves had to be made *kainos*—qualitatively different from what they were. The problem was not Jesus' message, but the receptacles into which it had to be poured. The new (*kainos*) wineskin of a softened heart was needed to receive the new (*neos*) truth of the gospel.

Jesus' ministry angered the Jewish leaders because, in the process of producing new wineskins capable of receiving God's new wine, it shattered the old legalistically molded vessels they had so carefully crafted.

This lesson portrays the disturbing impact of Jesus' *neos* ministry. As you study it, consider carefully whether you have been made *kainos.* Has the old worldly mold been broken and a new receptacle crafted capable of holding the eternal truths of God?

Calling the First Disciples
(Matthew 4:18–22; Mark 1:16–20; Luke 5:1–11)
Among the first vessels to be shattered were four fishermen living and working along the northern shore of the Sea of Galilee.

John, James, Andrew, and Simon had already attached themselves to Jesus as "part-time" disciples and readily responded to His challenging call to full-time ministry.

Scripture says they reacted to His "follow Me, and I will make you fishers of men" (Matthew 4:19) by immediately leaving their nets and following Him. Those few simple words describe a highly significant event in the lives of the four men. "Leaving their nets" meant walking away from a successful business that provided a good living with no intention of going back.

Jesus had gone to the sea that day specifically to recruit them, but as usual, He hadn't gone alone. A persistent throng of hungry hearers crowding Him ever closer to the water finally drove Him into Simon's fishing boat. From the boat, a little ways off shore, He finished teaching them, then turned to Simon and said, "Put out into the deep water and let down your nets for a catch" (Luke 5:4).

Simon, fighting the fatigue and discouragement of a long, unproductive night, obeyed—perhaps out of faith or perhaps only to humor Jesus. To his amazement, the nets quickly filled to the breaking point. Frantically, Simon and his crew signaled their partners on the shore for help, but even after splitting the catch, both boats seemed dangerously close to sinking.

Suddenly in the midst of all this chaos, understanding flashed in Simon's mind. He fell at Jesus' feet and cried, "Depart from me, for I am a sinful man, O Lord!" having just realized that if Jesus could see into the depths of the sea, He could also see into the depths of his soul (v. 8). The old vessel housing Simon's soul shattered. He was made *kainos,* qualitatively different from what he had been before and uniquely suited for the Master's work.

Not Exactly "Nine to Five"
(Matthew 8:14–17; Mark 1:21–39; Luke 4:31–44)

Jesus settled into a routine of teaching in the synagogue at Capernaum where His delivery of *neos* truth was received by astonished Jews unaccustomed to hearing rabbis teach on their own authority. On one particular Sabbath, their astonishment gave way to amazement as a demon-possessed man confronted Jesus in the synagogue.

The Bible gives no hint of any demon being unafraid of Jesus or refusing to submit to His authority, and the demon in the Capernaum synagogue was no exception. He cried out in the midst of Jesus' teaching, "What do we have to do with You, Jesus of Nazareth? Have You come to destroy us? I know who You are—the Holy One of God!" (Luke 4:34). Jesus responded with a decisive rebuke, "Be quiet and come out of him!" (v. 35), and the demon complied, leaving the bystanders in the synagogue awestruck at His power.

Following this encounter, Jesus and His disciples hastened to Simon's house where his mother-in-law lay ill with a high fever. Perhaps stimulated by the recent victory over the demon, the woman's relatives and friends implored Jesus to help her. Jesus touched her and rebuked the fever, exorcising the physical illness as thoroughly as He had the demon. The woman's healing was immediate and complete, allowing her to rise at once and resume her household duties.

Even though Jesus had not encouraged public discussion of His works, word spread quickly; and by sunset, people suffering from all kinds of physical, mental, and spiritual afflictions descended upon Simon's house. Jesus, motivated by divine compassion, cared for each one despite the lateness of the hour and the depth of His own fatigue.

The pace of Jesus' ministry was physically and spiritually exhausting, requiring Him to seek refreshment, rejuvenation, and direction in extended quiet times of prayer. He understood the necessity of separating Himself from the demands of the people so that He could clearly discern the will of God.

Miracles and Discourses
(Matthew 8:1–4; 9:1–17; 12:1–21; Mark 1:40–3:12; Luke 5:12–6:19)

As Jesus traveled, His notoriety increased. It was becoming increasingly difficult to remain neutral toward the itinerant preacher-healer from Galilee. His words and His deeds demanded a response—usually a passionate one. The people wanted Him for their king. The religious leaders wanted Him dead.

Jesus' escalating fame sharpened His emphasis on the true purpose of His ministry. He reminded the people that His kingdom was not of this world, and He refused to allow the religious leaders to harm Him before His time had come. His miracles and discourses underscore this emphasis.

The healing miracles demonstrate both His compassionate desire to relieve human suffering and His divine power to overcome the root of that suffering—sin itself. Jesus could have healed the leper's rotting body from a safe distance, but He reached out to touch him instead, touching his soul as well. Before He healed the paralytic, He forgave his sin. He attended a dinner party with notorious sinners and informed His critics He had not come to call the righteous, but sinners, to repentance. When He cast out demons, they acknowledged their defeat by identifying Him as the Son of God.

Matthew describes His healing ministry with the words of Isaiah's prophecy.

> Behold, My servant whom I have chosen;
> My beloved in whom My soul is well-pleased;
> I will put My Spirit upon Him,
> And He shall proclaim justice to the Gentiles.
> He will not quarrel, nor cry out;
> Nor will anyone hear His voice in the streets.
> A battered reed He will not break off,
> And a smoldering wick He will not put out,
> Until He leads justice to victory.
> And in His Name the Gentiles will hope.
> (Matthew 12:18–21)

Jesus' kingdom was not of this world, for He was not a political Messiah. He came to conquer sin, and His miracles validated His divine authority to do exactly that.

His discourses with the scribes and Pharisees in these portions of the Gospels highlight the escalating conflict that would eventually precipitate His death. The scribes who witnessed the healing of the paralytic and heard Jesus forgive his sins understood His blatant claim to be God in the flesh. When they labeled Him a glutton and a drunkard because He dined with sinners, He emphatically declared that their self-righteousness would deny them access to the very kingdom of God they claimed to represent.

When the Pharisees accused His disciples of breaking the Sabbath by plucking corn, Jesus denounced their disregard for the intended purpose of the day and declared Himself "Lord of the Sabbath" (v. 8). Finally, when their objection to His healing the man with a withered hand was angrily rebuffed, they "went out and immediately began taking counsel with the Herodians against Him, as to how they might destroy Him" (Mark 3:6). Little did they realize their actions had launched God's predetermined plan for His Son (Acts 2:23).

Jesus had come to fulfill Old Testament revelation, but He could not do it within the confines of their pseudo-Judaism. His systematic destruction of traditional legalism not only angered the leaders; it confused some of the elect. John's disciples came wanting to know why Jesus' disciples disregarded certain Jewish rituals, and Jesus answered them with parables. The friends of the bridegroom do not fast while the bridegroom is with them; new cloth is not used to patch old garments; and new wine cannot be contained in old wineskins. Those who had been molded in tradition must be shattered and made *kainos* before they could receive *neos* truth.

The Appointment of the Twelve
(Matthew 10:2–4; Mark 3:13–19; Luke 6:12–16;
Acts 1:13, 15–26)

The selection of twelve men from among His disciples to bear the responsibility of learning from Him and going out to preach weighed so heavily on the Messiah that He spent an entire night in prayer before making the decision. The selection of twelve was apparently intentional, and most likely symbolic of the new manifestation of God's covenant of grace, represented by the twelve apostles, superseding its old manifestation, represented by the twelve tribes.

The men themselves came from such varied backgrounds and diverse philosophies that only the catalytic presence of the Son of God in their midst could have bound and held them together. The group included prosperous businessmen, a hated tax collector, a political zealot, and a traitor, along with impetuous Simon Peter and thoughtful John.

The four listings of the apostles in the New Testament contain some revealing similarities and differences.

MATTHEW	MARK	LUKE	ACTS
Simon Peter	*Simon Peter*	*Simon Peter*	*Simon Peter*
Andrew	James	Andrew	James
James	John	James	John
John	Andrew	John	Andrew
Philip	*Philip*	*Philip*	*Philip*
Bartholomew	Bartholomew	Bartholomew	Thomas
Thomas	Matthew	Matthew	Bartholomew
Matthew	Thomas	Thomas	Matthew
James, the son of Alpheus	*James, the son of Alpheus*	*James, the son of Alpheus*	*James, the son of Alpheus*
Thaddeus	Thaddeus	Simon, the Zealot	Simon, the Zealot
Simon, the Canaean	Simon, the Canaean	Judas, the brother of James	Judas, the brother of James
Judas Iscariot	Judas Iscariot	Judas Iscariot	

Three distinct groups seem to have crystallized around the leadership of Simon Peter, Philip, and James, and the order in which the groups appear may reflect the closeness of their relationships with the Messiah. Simon Peter is always mentioned first, and Judas Iscariot last, reflecting Peter's eventual assumption of overall leadership of the group and Judas' eventual perfidy.

Some of the names on these lists are very familiar to us, and others are virtual strangers, but all shared in the glorious blessing of having lived and learned in close proximity to the Messiah. All but one of them had indeed been made *kainos* and would soon be given the opportunity to demonstrate their unique "re-creation" as vessels fit for the Master's use.

Notes

1. If you are not a Greek scholar (and my pastor continually reminds me that one semester of Greek doesn't make me a scholar—it only makes me dangerous!), ask your pastor, an elder of your church, or a trusted Christian bookseller to recommend a few reliable Greek reference tools to help you study God's Word.

2. Spiros Zodhiates, *The Complete Word Study Dictionary: New Testament* (Chattanooga, Tenn.: AMG Publishers, 1992), 1007.

Exercises

Review

1. On the map in appendix C, locate and mark the Sea of Galilee. Relocate and note the location of Capernaum on the northern shore of this sea. Consult a Bible atlas and/or other reference books, and find out all you can about the Sea of Galilee, for example, its size, characteristics, ability to support a fishing industry, sailing conditions, etc.

2. In your own words, explain the difference between the two Greek words translated "new" in the New Testament, *kainos* and *neos*. Why is understanding the distinction between these two words important to understanding the ministry of Jesus Christ?

3. Describe the method Jesus used to call His first four disciples to full-time ministry. Reread Luke 5:27–32 and describe any similarities between the method Jesus used to call Levi (Matthew) and the method He used to call the four fishermen. Do you see any connection between the way these men were called to follow Jesus and the way men and women are called to follow Him in our day? If so, explain.

4. Reread the primary Scripture passages listed at the outset of this lesson, and describe (citing specific examples) the way demons reacted to Jesus. Relate what you read about their re-

actions to Jesus in these passages to what is said about them in James 2:19. Are you able to draw any conclusions from these passages about the nature of saving faith? If so, explain.

5. Why were the Jewish leaders so upset by Jesus' ministry? Give some examples of how they responded to His ministry. How did Jesus' popularity with the people affect the way He conducted His ministry?

6. Describe any insights you gained into the ministry of Jesus by studying His choice of the twelve men who would be His apostles.

Application

1. Have you become a *kainos* vessel fit to receive Jesus' *neos* truth? If so, describe how you first became aware of this change in your life. What ongoing evidence do you see in your life of the reality of this change?

   If you do not believe you have been "made new," please read appendix A, "What Must I Do to Be Saved?" before going on to the next lesson, and ask God to help you understand it.

2. How does Jesus' call to the four fishermen and Levi to follow Him relate to the way He has called *you* to follow Him? Answer this question as specifically as you can.

Digging Deeper:

1. Using a concordance and any other biblical research tools at your disposal, write a biblically based definition of a "miracle." Then, survey the Bible and see if you can detect a pattern of miraculous events in Scripture. (That is, do miracles occur randomly throughout the Bible, or do they tend to cluster in certain time periods?) What conclusions can you draw about miracles from the pattern you detect? Now see if you detect any differences in the *types* of miracles that occur at different periods of biblical history. If so, what conclusions can you draw from these differences?

Primary Passages

Matthew 5–7; 11:20–30;
  12:22–45
Mark 3:20–35
Luke 7:1–8:3

Supplementary Passages

Matthew 11:2–19; 12:46–50
Luke 6:17–49; 8:19–21

Before reading the lesson material, please read the primary Scripture passages listed above and as many of the supplementary passages as time allows. Then briefly summarize in your notebook what you have read. (Do not go into detail. Limit your summary to whom the passages discuss, what is being discussed, and where and when the events in the passages occur.)

5

But I Say to You

*Jesus boldly set the authority of
His own word against that of any other.
He taught His disciples, challenged Pharisees,
encouraged a centurion, motivated a grieving mother,
reminded John the Baptist, permitted women,
and cautioned His own family—
to evaluate the words of the world
in the light of His own.
"You have heard that it was said. . . .
But I say to you . . ."*

On November 19, 1997, Kenny and Bobbi McCaughey of Carlisle, Iowa, made the front pages of most American newspapers by becoming the parents of a surprisingly healthy set of septuplets. All seven babies weighed in at more than two pounds and were given an excellent chance of survival by doctors who hailed their arrival as nothing short of miraculous.

The real miracle in the McCaughey family, however, has more to do with the condition of their souls than the condition of their babies. Kenny and Bobbi McCaughey are Christians who chose to act on the authority of Jesus Christ rather than on that of recognized medical experts. During the course of her pregnancy, Bobbi and Kenny were advised to abort some of the "fetuses" to give the others a better chance of survival.

However, the McCaugheys opted for prayer instead of "reduction" (the medical term for the advised procedure) and entrusted the welfare of Kenneth, Nathaniel, Brandon, Joel, Kelsey, Natalie, and Alexis to the sovereignty of God. Kenny's words summarized their commitment: "We're . . . waiting to see what happens and just trust that God's given us these babies. It's all in His hands."[1]

Kenny and Bobbi McCaughey remind me of the city set on a hill that Jesus described in the Sermon on the Mount. Their situation providentially thrust them into prominence. The eyes of the world were upon them that November—and the McCaugheys did not hide their light under a peck-measure. They deliberately set the light of their "good works" on a lampstand where it could clearly reflect the glory of God.

The effectiveness of their testimony stemmed from their willingness to base their decisions on the words of Scripture rather than the words of men. Jesus set this standard for the McCaugheys (and all other Christians) early in His ministry when He challenged those who heard Him speak to restructure their minds in accordance with His bold assertion, "You have heard that it was said. . . . But I say to you . . ."

Teaching the Disciples
(Matthew 5:1–7:29; Luke 6:17–49)

Whether you view Jesus' Sermon on the Mount as an all-at-once-delivered, ministry-launching sermon or as Matthew's masterful summary of Jesus' public teaching, you see in it a breathtaking panorama of the kingdom of God. When Jesus saw the multitudes, went up on the mountain, and opened His mouth to teach, He laid the authoritative foundation for the Christian faith, and demanded that we listen to Him instead of the world.

The sermon's introduction is a literary masterpiece in itself. Commonly known as *the Beatitudes,* it describes the regenerated character of those who inherit the kingdom of God. Heirs of the kingdom are *poor in spirit* because their eyes have been opened to their sinful inability to save themselves. They *mourn* over the sin that separates them from God and *humble* themselves under His absolute power.

God's gracious regeneration of their inner beings stimulates a *hunger and thirst for righteousness* that He alone can satisfy. Satisfaction of that thirst encourages them to share the *mercy* they have received, strive for *purity* of life, and bring *peace* to those around them.

The heirs of the kingdom know what it means to rejoice when they are *persecuted for righteousness sake*. As transient residents of a world that doesn't understand or appreciate them, they ground their joy in the assurance of God's unbreakable promises. He has forgiven their sin and blessed them with His constant comfort and strength. They exult in their status as children of God and look forward to spending eternity in His presence.

Jesus summarized the character of the heirs of the kingdom in two key words—"salt" and "light." As such, they exert a preserving and illuminating influence in our dark and decaying world, causing those who see their good works to glorify their Father in heaven.

Jesus called His followers to put off the legalistic trappings of religious ritualism and clothe themselves in the righteousness of God. Speaking on His own authority, He carefully distinguished the stifling traditions of the religious leaders from the eternal requirements of God's law, and exhorted His listeners to eschew the one and embrace the other.

Acting on Jesus' authoritative pronouncements would revolutionize their religious activities by shifting their focus from self to God. Those who absorbed themselves in the pursuit of the kingdom would store up treasure in heaven and escape the worldly snares of worry, vindictiveness, and selfishness. They would seek God's wisdom to follow the narrow path despised by the majority of mankind and to discern the erroneous doctrines of wolfish false teachers disguised in sheep's clothing.

Jesus closed His sermon by underscoring the heirs' complete dependence upon God in their pursuit of the kingdom. Those who sought entrance on their own merits would be turned away at the door by Jesus Himself. Only those who did the will of the Father would be admitted. Jesus' authoritative Word remains the only secure foundation for the Christian life; all else is treacherously shifting sand.

Encouraging a Centurion
(Matthew 8:5–13; Luke 7:1–10)

One of the more curious aspects of Jesus' ministry was its appeal to Gentiles. The Jews were an exclusive race, carefully guarding their genetic and spiritual purity against Gentile pollution. And they naturally expected their Messiah to do the same. Jesus, however, constantly astounded them by directing His authoritative pronouncements to Jew and Gentile alike.

The Jews' natural aversion to Gentiles in general and to Romans in particular highlights the exceptional character of one centurion living in Capernaum. Having endeared himself to the Jews by building them a synagogue, he later received their hearty endorsement when he appealed to Jesus to heal his beloved, dangerously ill servant.

Jesus set out for the centurion's home, only to be stopped in His tracks by the righteous Gentile's humility. "Lord, do not trouble Yourself further, for I am not worthy for You to come under my roof . . . but just say the word, and my servant will be healed" (Luke 7:6–7). The centurion understood authority and willingly submitted himself to the *superior* authority of Jesus.

Jesus marveled at the greatness of the centurion's faith and encouraged his desire to embrace Jesus' all-inclusive message of redemption. "And I say to you that many shall come from east and west, and recline at the table with Abraham, and Isaac, and Jacob, in the kingdom of heaven; but the sons of the kingdom shall be cast out into the outer darkness; in that place there shall be weeping and gnashing of teeth" (Matthew 8:11–12).

Motivating a Grieving Mother
(Luke 7:11–17)

Soon after healing the centurion's servant, Jesus and His disciples traveled to the city of Nain and were met by a funeral cortège as they neared the city. A poor widow had lost her only son and now faced the grim prospects of first-century life without the much-needed care of a male protector.

Little did she realize that her brief encounter with Jesus would rekindle her hope and joy in living. Moved with compassion, He approached her, told her not to weep, and then *touched the bier*—a ceremonial taboo resulting in defilement. This simple act proclaimed His authority over societal traditions and riveted her attention on His words.

He then demonstrated His authority by raising the young man from the dead and restoring him to his mother. The full import of the drama playing out in front of them was not lost on the crowd surrounding the ecstatic little family. Luke tells us they glorified God, saying, "A great prophet has arisen among us," and, "God has visited His people!" (v. 16). Then they dispersed to spread the story throughout Judea and the surrounding area.

Reminding John the Baptist
(Matthew 11:2–30; Luke 7:18–35)

The disciples of John the Baptist were keeping close tabs on the escalating ministry of Jesus Christ—and for a very good reason. Since their leader's imprisonment, their regular reports were his only link to the One he had so effectively proclaimed. Despite their attempts to buoy his spirits, the longer John sat in his dismal cell, cut off from the fresh air and sunlight in which he had thrived, the more discouraged and depressed he became.

As he listened to his disciples describe Jesus' activities, He must have wondered why he, the herald, had not been miraculously delivered. Had he been wrong? Had he missed the Messiah? He had to know. Characteristically opting for the direct approach, he dispatched his disciples to ask Jesus point blank, "Are You the Expected One, or do we look for someone else?" (Luke 7:20).

Jesus' response was uncritically sympathetic. As John's disciples watched, He performed many wondrous signs and then sent them back to their leader with a reassuring reminder, "Go and report to John what you have seen and heard: the blind receive sight, the lame walk, the lepers are cleansed, and the deaf hear, the dead are raised up, the poor have the gospel preached to them. And blessed is he who keeps from stumbling over Me" (vv. 22–23). Jesus thus reminded John that the authority to do the things He did could only come from God. He had not been wrong, and he had indeed heralded the Messiah. By relying on the words of Jesus rather than his own bleak thinking, he could be saved from stumbling over the very One who had come to lift him up.

And "lift him up" He did. He chided those who criticized John, proclaiming, "Among those born of women, there is no one greater than John; yet he who is least in the kingdom of God is greater than he" (v. 28). As the one prophet privileged to see the One about whom he prophesied, John certainly qualified for greatness. Yet his greatness fell short of those who would enjoy the continual indwelling of His Spirit.

Jesus reinforced His exaltation of the herald by describing the kingdom of God as a powerful force advancing through the determined efforts of men like John. He admonished the crowd for its whimsicality, likening them to spoiled children who petulantly refuse to appreciate all efforts made in their behalf.

Matthew adds His pronouncement of "woes" upon the cities of Chorazin, Bethsaida, and Capernaum, who, having been exposed to great light, chose to remain in darkness. His words contain both a warning and a hope. Those who refused to submit to Jesus' indisputable display of authority would share the fate of those cursed cities, while those who accepted His yoke of authority would find present comfort and eternal rest for their souls.

Challenging Some Pharisees
(Matthew 12:22–45; Mark 3:20–30; Luke 7:36–50)

Jesus' popularity with the people and His authoritative teaching style continued to fuel the antagonism in the hearts of the tradition-bound Pharisees, many of whom freely expressed their contempt for His "inferior" social standing. One particular Pharisee named Simon has been immortalized in Scripture for just such behavior.

Simon extended to Jesus an apparent honor by inviting Him home for dinner, but contemptuously neglected to extend the common courtesies of foot washing and anointing. Jesus made no mention of the obvious slight until a woman of scandalous reputation quietly entered the dining hall and fell at His feet, washing them with her tears and anointing them with precious ointment. As the fragrant aroma filled the room, Simon's face no doubt reflected his scornful thoughts about this "upstart Messiah." *If He really is a prophet, He would never let such a woman touch Him!*

Jesus seized the moment to confront the sanctimonious Pharisee with an authoritative presentation of eternal truth. Using a simple story followed by even simpler questions, Jesus proclaimed essentially the same message He had taught His disciples in the Sermon on the Mount. God's gracious forgiveness appeals only to those self-acknowledged sinners whose "poverty of spirit" enables them to recognize and mourn over their separation from God and to respond in humble love to His mercy. The self-righteous recognize no such need within themselves and therefore fail to respond humbly to God.

Simon wasn't the only Pharisee Jesus challenged with His authority. Several more reacted to His healing of a blind, mute demoniac by desperately attempting to discredit Him. Hearing the multitudes refer to Him as the promised Son of David, they feared a successful political move by a popular Messiah that would destroy their position and influence under Roman rule. Since Jesus' popularity seemed tied to His indisputable authority, perhaps His downfall could be effected through discrediting Him. What better way to extinguish this rising star than to align Him with Satan?

Jesus would prove difficult to discredit, however. He deflected their attempt with a stunning rebuttal. If He were Satan, would He "divide his own house" by casting out His own demons? And if He cast out demons by the power of Satan, by whose power did the Pharisees cast them out? If, however, Jesus' power came from God, then His claims had to be true. Only the power of God can bind the strong man, Satan, and plunder his house.

Condemning the Pharisees for attributing the work of the Holy Spirit to Satan, Jesus declared their sin unforgivable because it generated no repentance. Some of the scribes and Pharisees, scrambling to save face, demanded a "sign," to which Jesus responded with a scathing denunciation of their self-righteousness. While the men of Ninevah had repented at the preaching of Jonah, and the Queen of the South had responded to the wisdom of Solomon, the Pharisees had turned deaf ears and stony hearts to the incarnate Son of God. And their actions had sealed their doom. They stood hopeless and helpless before their Creator, unrepentant and thereby condemned.

Permitting the Women
(Luke 8:1–3)

One of the most outstanding examples of Jesus' distinctive authority was His exceptional regard for women. In a society that treated women as little more than possessions, Jesus' unprecedented respect for them set Him apart as a teacher like no other. Jesus permitted women equal access to the kingdom and always received them as full-fledged citizens.

Many women actually traveled with Jesus while others supported His ministry out of their private resources. Luke mentions three notable ladies in chapter 8 of his gospel: Mary Magdalene, who had been delivered from seven demons; Joanna, the wife of one of Herod's stewards; and Susanna, about whom he gives no details.

Cautioning the Family
(Matthew 12:46–50; Mark 3:31–35; Luke 8:19–21)

Scripture doesn't tell us why Jesus' mother and brothers came looking for Him while He was teaching and preaching. Perhaps they had heard so many conflicting and confusing stories about Him, they were concerned about His safety—or His sanity. Or perhaps they were fearful that His bold assertion of authority would bring disaster upon Him—and them. His response cautioned them to remember who He was and why He had come: "Who is my mother and who are My brothers? . . . Behold, My mother and My brothers! For whoever does the will of My Father who is in heaven, he is My brother and sister and mother" (Matthew 12:48–50).

The kingdom of God in their midst had redefined all things, even the concept of family. Mortal ties had been superseded by heavenly ones. "Blood" relatives must yield first place in the heart to spiritual kin. Jesus' remarks were not intended to repudiate His earthly family, but to affirm the spiritual family of those who had been born again by the power of the Holy Spirit.

Notes

1. R. Albert Mohler, "No Room in the Womb?" *World Magazine,* 15 November 1997, 21. Some details of the McCaugheys' story were taken from *The Albuquerque Journal,* 20 November 1997.

Exercises

Review

1. On the map in appendix C, locate and mark the cities of Nain, Chorazin, and Bethsaida. Note once more the location of Capernaum, and see if you determine the distance between Capernaum and Nain.

2. Reread Matthew 5:1–7:29 and write a "purpose statement" for the Sermon on the Mount. (Hint: In one sentence, explain why Jesus delivered [what He was trying to accomplish] this sermon.) Now, outline the sermon in a way that will help you remember its content. From your outline, briefly describe the major *themes* of the sermon. (Hint: Themes are topics an author discusses to accomplish his or her purpose(s) for writing.)

3. Reread Luke 7:1–17 and describe the similarities and differences in the way Jesus responded to the centurion and the widow. What lessons about Jesus' authority can you learn from His interaction with these two people?

4. Why did John send his disciples to Jesus? How did Jesus respond to them?

5. Reread Luke 7:36–50 and Matthew 12:22–45. What basic attitude stimulated the response of the Pharisees described in these passages? How did Jesus' response to them differ from the way He responded to the centurion, the widow, and John the Baptist?

6. Review the way Jesus responded to each person or group included in this lesson, and explain how each response exalts His authority over the words and wisdom of the world.

Application

1. Consider the way in which Jesus asserted His authority in the lives of the following people and prayerfully determine how each person's response to His assertion encourages, convicts, or exhorts you to submit specific areas of your own life to His authority. (Remember the tests of a specific application! Does it answer the questions Who? What? When? Where? and How?)

the disciples:
the centurion:
the widow:
John the Baptist:
the Pharisees:
women in general:
His family:

Digging Deeper:

1. In Matthew 12:31–32, Jesus mentions what is commonly referred to as "the unpardonable sin." Using a concordance and other reliable reference books at your disposal, do sufficient biblical research to answer the following questions and to explain your answers fully: (1) Exactly what is the unpardonable

sin? (2) Is it possible for a Christian to commit this sin? After you have completed your research and answered these questions, make an appointment with your pastor or one of your church's elders to discuss your conclusions.

2. Using a concordance and a Bible encyclopedia, find out all you can about the cities of Tyre, Sidon, Sodom, Chorazin, Bethsaida, and Capernaum. Based upon what you have learned about these cities, explain Jesus' pronouncement of woe on some of these cities in Matthew 11:21–24.

Primary Passages

Matthew 9:35–38; 10:5–11:1;
8:18, 23–34; 9:18–34;
Mark 5:1–43; 6:14–34
John 5:1–47

Supplementary Passages

Matthew 13:1–53; 14:13–36
14:1–12
Mark 4:1–41; 6:7–13, 35–56
Luke 8:4–18; 22–56; 9:1–17
John 6:1–21
Isaiah 6:1–13

Before reading the lesson material, please read the primary Scripture passages listed above and as many of the supplementary passages as time allows. Then briefly summarize in your notebook what you have read. (Do not go into detail. Limit your summary to whom the passages discuss, what is being discussed, and where and when the events in the passages occur.)

6

Eyes That See and Ears That Hear

Not all who heard Jesus teach
responded in faith.
Some ignored Him.
Some despised Him.
Some plotted to kill Him.
Others who heard Him teach
believed Him, loved Him,
and followed Him.
What made the difference?
Eyes that see and ears that hear.

"If you build it, they will come."

That's all it took in the nostalgic baseball movie *Field of Dreams*. But is it enough in Christian ministry? Absolutely not.

Faithfully presenting the gospel message isn't enough to bring unbelievers to saving faith. Faithfully preaching the truths of Scripture isn't enough to stimulate congregations to apply them. And faithfully living the Christian life isn't enough to usher in the new heaven and new earth.

Christian ministry is a privileged responsibility that ultimately depends upon *God's work,* not ours, to produce results. God doesn't need us to get His work done, even though He graciously uses us to accomplish His purposes. Our effectiveness in His service doesn't depend on our ability, cleverness, or persuasiveness, but rather on our willingness to acknowledge His sovereignty, submit to His will, and display His glory.

As we follow the ministry of Jesus in this lesson, we will be reminded, in several different ways, of our own inability to effect spiritual change in anyone's life. Spiritual change requires "eyes that see and ears that hear"—a spiritual responsiveness that comes only through God's gracious work in human hearts.

Reminded by Parables
(Matthew 13:1–53; Mark 4:1–34; Luke 8:4–18)

Effective teachers have long understood the value of analogies, and Jesus, the master teacher, was no exception. He routinely used parables[1] to communicate eternal truth to those God had blessed with spiritual responsiveness. His disciples at one point questioned His methods and received a response from the words of Isaiah.

> You will keep on hearing, but will not understand;
> And you will keep on seeing, but will not perceive;
> For the heart of this people has become dull,
> And with their ears they scarcely hear,
> And they have closed their eyes
> Lest they should see with their eyes,
> And hear with their ears,
> And understand with their heart and return,
> And I should heal them.
> (Matthew 13:14–15)

Parables, Jesus assured them, were an essential means of communicating truth to divinely prepared hearts while hiding it from those who have no part in the kingdom.

The parable of the sower vividly illustrates this fact by comparing the "soil" of the heart with the soil of Palestine. Not all seed that falls to the ground produces fruit, just as not all teaching that falls on the ear produces understanding. As the condition of the soil determines quality of growth, so the condition of the heart determines quality of comprehension.

Having established the basis for understanding parables, Jesus proceeded to offer a few more. The parable of the wheat and tares illustrates the difficulty of differentiating between true and false disciples in the early stages of growth. The parables of the mustard seed and leaven describe the pervasiveness of Christianity. And the parables of the hidden treasure and the pearl of great price highlight the incomparable value of the gospel.

Jesus also compared God's Final Judgment with a dragnet that hauls in a diverse assortment of fish, weeds, rocks, and junk that must be sorted out by fishermen on the shore. In a similar way, the gospel attracts an amazing variety of false and true "professors" who will be separated by God's angel's at the Final Judgment.

Jesus paused to ask His disciples if they understood His teaching and, after receiving their affirmative reply, directed one last parable specifically to them: "Therefore every scribe who has become a disciple of the kingdom of heaven is like a head of a household, who brings forth out of his treasure things new and old" (v. 51). Jesus seems to be reminding them of their regenerate ability to understand the continuity between old and new revelation and of their consequent responsibility to pass that understanding on to others.

Reminded by Miracles
(Matthew 8:23–34; 9:18–38; Mark 4:35–5:43; Luke 8:22–56)
The sudden storms that periodically churned the Sea of Galilee into a swirling caldron frequently caught even seasoned fishermen, like Jesus' disciples, off guard and left them frantically fighting for their lives. On one such occasion panic gave way to sheer irrationality as they shook the exhausted Son of God awake and cried, "Save us, Lord; we are perishing!" (Matthew 8:25). Jesus, distressed by the timidity of their faith, rebuked them *and* the storm, generating immediate compliance from the forces of nature and awe-struck astonishment from the chagrined fishermen.

I sometimes wonder if Jesus went right back to sleep as His stunned disciples pursued their course on the now eerily calm water. But if He did, He would soon be awakened again—this time by the blood-curdling cries of two demoniacs racing from their home in the tombs to accost the boat on the shore.

Scripture does not record the reaction of the disciples to this bone-chilling welcome, but they must have been every bit as terrified as they were by the storm. They had learned their lesson, however, and resolutely stood their ground—squarely behind Jesus!

As it turned out, that was the safest place to be. The legion of demonic forces afflicting the two men were no match for the Lord of the universe. They readily acknowledged Jesus' supreme authority and begged Him not to consign them to the abyss "before the time" (v. 29). Granting their request to send them into a herd of swine instead sparked a stampede that sent the entire herd hurtling over a cliff into the Sea of Galilee.

The frightened townspeople took one look at the huge "pig pile" in its watery grave and begged Jesus not to enter their city, while at least one of the restored demoniacs begged with equal fervency to be permitted to follow Him. Jesus skirted the town but sent His newest follower back to testify among them concerning "what great things the Lord has done for you, and how He had mercy on you" (Mark 5:19).

More miracles followed close on the heels of these two. A woman was healed of a long-standing medical problem, two blind men received their sight, a mute man regained the power of speech, and a young girl was raised from her death bed and restored to her grieving family.

The miracles recorded in these Gospel passages remind us again of our complete dependence on Jesus' sovereignty over natural forces, demonic spirits, physical afflictions, and death. He who (along with the Father and the Holy Spirit) created and sustains all things, equips, protects, and guides us in ministry. Without Him, we can do nothing.

Reminded by Declaration
(John 5:1–47)
While Jesus was in Jerusalem for a feast of the Jews, He passed by the Pool of Bethesda where scores of Jerusalem's physically

afflicted crowded each day hoping to be healed. Jesus' compassionate attention was arrested by a man whose affliction had disabled him for thirty-eight years. "Do you wish to get well?" Jesus inquired, to which the man responded, "Sir, I have no man to put me into the pool when the water is stirred up" (vv. 6–7).

"Arise, take up your pallet, and walk," Jesus told him (v. 8), reminding us of our own ministry-crippling sinfulness that is overcome only by hearing and heeding the voice of our Savior.

Jesus' proclivity for healing on the Sabbath continued to irritate the Jewish leaders. Their legalistic commitment to their own traditionalism prevented them from recognizing the very God who had instituted the Sabbath in the first place. Others just like them had obliterated His intended purpose for Sabbath observance centuries before. Because they possessed neither eyes to see nor ears to hear, they failed to understand His reiteration of that purpose now.

Jesus confronted their depraved unresponsiveness with a bold declaration of His equality with the Father. The truth of Jesus' testimony was supported by a fourfold witness surpassing the "two or three witnesses" required by their own Jewish law. Their obstinance in the face of clear testimony from John the Baptist, Jesus' works, God Himself, and the Holy Scripture condemned them as among those having no part in the kingdom of heaven.

Reminded by the Disciples
(Matthew 9:36–11:1; Mark 6:7–13, 30–32; Luke 9:1–6, 10)
Jesus never sugar-coated the cost of discipleship. He made sure His disciples understood their complete inability to function outside of divine enabling. As He scattered them across the rugged Galilean countryside to preach and teach in His name, He reminded them that effective Christian ministry required selfless devotion.

As His representatives, they should expect to be treated the way He had been treated. They would be received by some, ignored by others, and rejected by many. Persecution would be routine. They would be hauled before judges, thrown into prison, and scorned by their families. They would feel isolated, frustrated, and out of step with the world.

They would have to be "shrewd as serpents, and innocent as doves" (Matthew 10:16), alert and responsive to ministry opportunities and hazards while maintaining purity in their motives and attitudes. They would walk a fearsome pathway, but would have no need to fear, because they would not go alone. The Holy Spirit would go with them to inspire their speech and guide their actions.

Jesus sent them out two by two with instructions to move efficiently and minister purposefully. They were not to weigh themselves down with provisions but to trust God to provide through the generosity of others. They were sent to the "lost sheep of the house of Israel" (v. 6) to seek out the receptive and bypass the rejecters. They were told to give freely what they had been freely given and to expect nothing in return.

When they returned, flushed with success and eager to report every detail of their mission, Jesus called them aside for rest and reflection. In so doing, He taught them that productive ministry requires periods of repose. God, in His wisdom, houses His Holy Spirit in weak earthen vessels that require frequent rejuvenation and repair. Ministering in such weakness highlights God's strength and underscores our complete dependence on Him.

Reminded by the Death of John
(Matthew 14:1–12; Mark 6:14–29; Luke 9:7–9)

Scripture records scores of reactions to the ministry of Jesus, and one of the most tragic was that of King Herod. Haunted by guilt over the brutal murder of John the Baptist, he read into the miraculous activities of Jesus a return of the slain prophet to torment him.

John, in true prophetic fashion, had challenged Herod concerning his marital sins despite dire personal consequences. Herod, defending his "political right" to marry his brother's wife and disregarding the moral ramifications of his actions, removed the public embarrassment of his relentless nemesis by throwing him into prison. Herodias, the woman scorned, lobbied for John's death, but Herod, strangely intrigued by his eccentric prisoner and fearing the reaction of the people, refused to comply.

Herodias was not easily dissuaded, however, and capitalized on Herod's licentiousness to pull off the dastardly deed. The king would never know another day of peace. Because he had neither eyes to see nor ears to hear, his sin was beyond expiation and his soul beyond hope.

Reminded by a Transformation
(Matthew 14:13–21; Mark 6:33–44; Luke 9:11–17;
John 6:1–14)
The multitudes who persistently dogged Jesus' heels presented His disciples with some interesting logistical problems, not the least of which was meals. In the days before "Golden Arches" and specialized catering services, feeding large groups of people in the great outdoors was quite a challenge.

On one such occasion, Jesus' compassionate nature and teacher's mentality joined forces to reinforce, once again, His disciples' utter dependence upon Him. Seeing a crowd of perhaps ten to fifteen thousand people rapidly closing around them, Jesus charged His men with the responsibility of feeding them.

Responding as true earthen vessels, they protested, "Lord, on our budget we can't possibly feed a crowd this size. Send them home to eat" (my paraphrase). Jesus readily granted their assessment of their own inadequacy but completely ignored their suggested solution. Instead He sent them scurrying to determine the extent of their available resources and displayed His own complete sufficiency by transforming their insufficient offering to more than meet the need.

What a lesson for them and for all Christians through the ages! No matter how great or small our own personal resources may be, they are always insufficient in themselves to accomplish the purposes of God. Before they can be used in effective Christian ministry, they must be offered to Him in faith and used in confident expectation of His transforming power.

Reminded by Our Fears
(Matthew 14:22–33; Mark 6:45–52; John 6:15–21)
Jesus performed miracles to validate His authority to minister as He did, but those without eyes to see and ears to hear never re-

ally understood. Many of those who had been fed miraculously fell into that category and saw in Jesus, not the perfect Redeemer, but the perfect provider. Spurred on by greedy self-interest, they launched a campaign to make Him their king. Jesus, reading their hearts and rejecting their schemes, dismissed the crowd, dispatched the disciples across the lake, and retired to the mountain to pray.

Alfred Edersheim, in his classic *Life and Times of Jesus the Messiah,* draws on Mark's account of this incident to paint a beautiful word picture of the Savior deep in prayer, suddenly looking up from His mountain vantage point to see His beloved disciples struggling to stay afloat in their tiny craft in yet another of Galilee's notorious squalls. What a vivid reminder of the Savior's constant watchful care over *all* His beloved disciples throughout the ages!

Sensing their distress, He immediately went to their aid, walking over the water toward them. The disciples, obviously not expecting such an unusual rescue, reacted in terror to His "ghostly" approach. His reassuring, "Take courage, it is I; do not be afraid" (Matthew 14:27) calmed their quaking hearts and stimulated an eager Peter to request permission to meet Jesus *on the water*. I can easily imagine a grin on the face of the Savior as He replied, "Come!" (v. 29).

Peter's experience is an excellent object lesson for us all. He impetuously asked the Lord to allow Him to do the impossible, fixed his eyes firmly on His Savior and stepped out in faith. Then, right in the middle of accomplishing the task, he allowed himself to be distracted by terrifying circumstances. As his eyes strayed from Jesus, he was immediately overwhelmed by wind, rain, water, and human inadequacy—and sank like a rock.

Peter, however, was not without resources. He had all he needed to deal with that horrible sinking feeling because he had been blessed with eyes to see and ears to hear. "Lord, save me!" he cried (v. 30) and was not disappointed.

God always calls His elect to do the impossible and then equips them to do it. Sometimes in our exuberant desire to serve, we forget where our sufficiency lies. But even then, Jesus is quick to forgive and restore. All it takes is repentant, confessional prayer.

If we call Him, He will come.

Notes

1. Parables differ from allegories in that they are used to teach one primary point. Thus, each element in a parable cannot be understood to "stand for" multiple teaching points. Pushing the interpretation of a parable beyond its primary intent is a dangerous practice that must be avoided. For more information about interpreting parables, see lesson 5 of *Turning On the Light.*

Exercises

Review

1. Review the map in appendix C to refresh your memory regarding the location of Galilee, Jerusalem, and the travel routes between them.

2. Describe the main point of each of the following parables:

   parable of the sower:
   parable of the wheat and tares:
   parables of the mustard seed and leaven:
   parables of the hidden treasure and the pearl of great price:
   parable of the dragnet:

3. Consider all the miracles of Jesus we have studied so far and indicate which ones demonstrate His sovereignty over each of the following areas:

   natural forces:
   demonic forces:
   physical afflictions:
   death:

   Why is it important and necessary for Jesus to display His sovereignty in this way?

4. Reread Matthew 9:36–11:1 and explain why it was important for the disciples to be reminded of their dependence upon Christ's sufficiency before they embarked on their first ministry adventure. Then explain why Christ taught them about God's purposes for rest when they returned.

5. Describe how those who have eyes to see and ears to hear respond differently to Jesus than do those who do not have eyes to see and ears to hear. Use specific examples from this lesson to illustrate your answer.

6. What did Peter learn from his "sinking spell"? Why is this lesson important for all Christians?

Application

1. When did you first become aware that you had "eyes to see and ears to hear." Describe how your interest in and response to spiritual issues changed as a result of this transformation. Use specific examples.

2. Describe your primary ministry activities. In what specific ways are you, in these activities, particularly dependent upon God's power to minister effectively? In what specific ways are you usually tempted to minister in your own strength instead of in reliance upon God? How does He usually convict you about this sin?

Digging Deeper

1. Study Genesis 1–3, paying particular attention to Genesis 2:1–3, along with Exodus 20:1–17 and Deuteronomy 5:1–27, and consider the following question: Is "keeping the Sabbath" a Creation ordinance (that is, part of the created order of things and therefore an essential, ongoing element in God's design for humanity). If so, how does its designation as a Creation ordinance affect *your* observance of it? Consult with your pastor or an elder of your church for recommended reading and/or assistance in answering this question.

2. Kenneth Wuest, in his *Word Studies in the Greek New Testament,* cautions us, "No parable walks on all fours, but will limp somewhere if the expositor seeks to explain every detail." Using sound biblical reference tools, research the topic of parables and explain what Wuest means by this statement. Give some examples to illustrate his meaning.

Primary Passages	**Supplementary Passages**
Matthew 15:21–17:13	Matthew 15:1–20; 17:14–21
Mark 7:1–23, 31–37; 8:22–26;	Mark 7:24–30; 8:1–21, 27–38
9:2–29	Luke 9:18–43
John 6:22–71	2 Peter 1:17–18

Before reading the lesson material, please read the primary Scripture passages listed above and as many of the supplementary passages as time allows. Then briefly summarize in your notebook what you have read. (Do not go into detail. Limit your summary to whom the passages discuss, what is being discussed, and where and when the events in the passages occur.)

7

The Bread of Life

The Man who fed the multitudes
claimed equality with God.
His compassion filled their empty stomachs,
and His teaching filled their empty souls.
He reached beyond their temporal cares,
and pointed them toward heaven.
He knew their need for earthly bread
disguised one so much greater.
They could not live on bread alone.
they needed
the Bread of Life.

Yesterday afternoon I opened my office door and stepped into a hallway filled with the mouth-watering aroma of baking bread. Almost immediately my stomach dispatched an urgent "Feed me!" signal to my brain, even though I wasn't the least bit hungry before I opened the door. My sudden, overwhelming desire for bread had been stimulated solely by the enticing fragrance permeating the hallway.

Perhaps the apostle Paul was thinking about these sense-quickening qualities of freshly baked bread when he wrote,

But thanks be to God, who always leads us in His triumph in Christ, and manifests through us the sweet aroma of the knowledge of Him in every place. For we are a fragrance of Christ to God among those who are being saved and among those who are perishing; to the one an aroma from death to death, to the other an aroma from life to life. (2 Corinthians 2:14–16)

His words remind us that we, as the body of Christ in the world, should fill God's nostrils with the pleasant aroma of our witness in His service. What strikes me about this passage is that the pleasing aroma arises from *our witness,* not from the world's response to our witness. The aroma "from death to death" smells no different to God than the aroma "from life to life" since both emanate from faithful testimony regarding His glorious plan of salvation.

Lesson 7 focuses on Jesus as the "Bread of Life," the fragrant nutrient essential for creating and sustaining spiritual life in fallen humanity. Everywhere Jesus went, the aroma of the gospel followed Him. Many people were immediately drawn to it, while many others were repelled. But God delighted in the scent penetrating heaven and earth as Jesus testified perfectly of His Father's great plan.

"I Am the Bread of Life"
(John 6:22–71)
John opens his account of Jesus' well-known Bread of Life discourse with an almost humorous chase scene spotlighting the miraculously fed multitudes in hot pursuit of their "meal ticket" around the Sea of Galilee. They finally caught up with Him "on the other side of the sea," only to have their breakfast plans completely scrambled. Jesus confronted their temporal-mindedness and checked their salivating desire for earthly bread with a mystifying description of Himself as the bread of God that "comes down out of heaven, and gives life to the world" (v. 33).

They were foolish, He said, to work so hard for "food which

perishes" when the "food which endures to eternal life" was within such easy reach (v. 27). John's scene then shifts from comic to tragic as the multitudes demonstrated their utter lack of comprehension with grumbling words and faithless actions.

Why did they miss His point? Jesus tells us in verses 35–65, a passage that defines the great foundational truths of election, irresistible grace, perseverance, and by implication, the utter depravity of man. The multitudes missed His point because their "natural" hunger reflected their unredeemed, depraved desires. Spiritual hunger is generated by God and found only in the elect (v. 65). Those who hunger and thirst after righteousness do not resist the filling of His grace (v. 37), and having been filled, they are sustained and raised up on the last day (vv. 40, 44).

The stark distinction between the lost and the elect is vividly portrayed in John's final scene. As the multitudes drifted away unfilled and unsatisfied, Jesus turned to the few who remained and asked, "You do not want to go away also, do you?" (v. 67). Peter responded not only for that small group but for the redeemed of the ages when he said, "Lord, to whom shall we go? You have the words of eternal life" (v. 68).

The Discourse in the Synagogue
(Matthew 15:1–20; Mark 7:1–23)

The aroma of the Bread of Life wafting through the synagogue in Jerusalem had become downright noxious to the Jewish leaders and incited them to launch yet another attempt to discredit Jesus and His ministry. Confronting Him on the issue of purification and washings, they accused His disciples of not walking "according to the tradition of the elders" (Mark 7:5) when they ate bread with unwashed hands.

Jesus condemned their hypocritical elevation of human tradition above God's law by identifying them as the subjects of Isaiah's prophesy: "This people honors Me with their lips, but their heart is far from Me, but in vain do they worship Me, teaching as doctrines the precepts of men" (vv. 6–7). And just in case they missed the point, He followed-up with a "real life" example of their sin—the popular practice of declaring material possessions *Corban* in order to escape legal responsibility for their aging parents.

He then called the multitudes to Himself and countered the teaching of their "blind guides" by explaining that true defilement always comes from the sinful human heart, not from physical contact with material substances.

Healings in Tyre, Sidon, and Decapolis
(Matthew 15:21–38; Mark 7:24–8:9)

Jesus carefully controlled His confrontations with the Jewish leaders in order to carry out God's plan. Therefore, following the angry encounter in the Jerusalem synagogue, He gathered His disciples and departed for the gentile regions of Tyre and Sidon. There He encountered a Syro-Phoenician woman who persistently beseeched Him to help her demon-possessed daughter.

Jesus, sensing the genuineness of her faith, seized the opportunity to put the finishing touches on the portrait of the gospel He had begun painting by the well in Samaria. Even though He had been sent to "the lost sheep of the house of Israel" (Matthew 15:24), the message of salvation would encompass Jew, Samaritan, and Gentile alike. The Samaritan prostitute and this Syro-Phoenician mother had both been chosen to share in the inheritance of the saints in light, and their faith stands immortalized in the pages of God's Book.

After leaving Tyre and Sidon, Jesus and His disciples traveled once again to Galilee where the Bread of Life continued to quicken and sustain the sorely afflicted. Matthew records the healing of the lame, blind, mute, maimed, and many others, while Mark focuses on the healing of one deaf-mute man. The physical contact associated with these miracles provides further evidence of the compassion and concern that were such an integral part of Jesus' devotion to doing His Father's will.

Jesus then fed another great multitude in much the same way He had done before. Matthew and Mark humbly emphasize the amazing ability of the disciples to lose sight of God's gracious provision from one crisis to the next. They remind us of our own tendency to do the same. We, like those disciples, are sinfully slow to run to Jesus with a problem exactly like one He has already solved for us.

Critical Issues
(Matthew 15:39–16:28; Mark 8:10–9:1; Luke 9:18–27)

Jesus knew His time on earth was growing short, and He intensified His efforts to teach His disciples the essential truths they needed to grasp before His departure. He emphasized the subtle dangers lurking in their tradition-bound religious system by warning them to beware of the leaven of the Pharisees and Sadducees who were always looking for a sign. As a permeating influence, leaven served Jesus well to illustrate the pervasive corruption inherent in worldly thinking.

His disciples would have to guard against such influences while striving to remember their rich resources in the Bread of Life. Could it be that His reference to their concern over having no bread was an allusion to the time when He would no longer be with them? If so, the words that follow glow with assurance. His abundant provision of their needs in the past afforded them equally abundant reason to trust Him in the future.

Mark's exclusive account of the healing of the blind man *in stages* leaves us in some doubt about whether the disciples were present; but if they were, Jesus may have been cautioning them about expecting full spiritual maturity and strength *all at once*. Perhaps He was picturing for them the progressive stages of sanctification that would culminate in perfection only in heaven.

The landmark discussion in Caesarea Philippi between Jesus and His disciples highlighted the central issue of Christianity: the identity of Jesus Christ. His soul-piercing question "Who do you say that I am?" (Matthew 16:15) brought the little group face to face with the world-shaking importance of the mission to which they had been called.

Peter's impetuous, forthright answer flowed not from his own powers of reason, but from the God to whom he had committed his life. Jesus' response validated its source—and its truthfulness.

> Blessed are you, Simon Barjona, because flesh and blood
> did not reveal this to you, but My Father who is in heaven.
> And I also say to you that you are Peter, and upon this
> rock I will build My church; and the gates of Hades shall
> not overpower it. I will give you the keys of the kingdom
> of heaven; and whatever you shall bind on earth shall be
> bound in heaven, and whatever you shall loose on earth
> shall be loosed in heaven. (vv. 17–19)

Jesus' designation of Peter as the first official leader of His
church was, without doubt, an awesome blessing, but it was also
a grave responsibility. Those who lead Christ's church join Peter
in confessing the truth about Christ and bear much of the brunt
of Satan's attacks against God's impregnable fortress. Having
taken the point position, they are expected to exercise properly
the "keys of the kingdom," binding and loosing on earth what has
already been bound and loosed in heaven.

It was an awesome responsibility thrust upon Peter with little
or no warning—and it's really no wonder he immediately stumbled under the load. Peter "naturally" misconstrued his leadership role as one of protector-defender and leaped boldly into action when Jesus mentioned His impending death. I believe Peter's
intentions were good and that he didn't see Satan's second major
temptation of Jesus cleverly veiled in his words. Jesus, however,
recognized it immediately. His decisive rebuke of Satan served also
to correct Peter, making it clear to him and to all who would follow him that God's purposes can only be accomplished by use
of His means.

Jesus followed the correction with a call to commitment that
clearly defined the radical nature of Christian conversion: "If anyone wishes to come after Me, let him deny himself, and take up
his cross daily, and follow Me. For whoever wishes to save his life
shall lose it; but whoever loses his life for My sake, he is the one
who will save it. For what is a man profited if he gains the whole
world, and loses or forfeits himself?" (Luke 9:23–25).

This watershed statement describes the glorious transformation of those who partake of the Bread of Life. The pursuer of the
world is crucified on the cross of self-denial, and the pursuer of

righteousness is raised to walk in newness of life. Only those who die to self will know the joy of eternal life in Christ.

The Transfiguration
(Matthew 17:1–13; Mark 9:2–13; Luke 9:28–36)

Jesus' transfiguration gloriously revealed His deity to the three key leaders of the men who would soon be entrusted with the keys of the kingdom. Awe-struck and astonished, they would have joyfully camped on the mount for all eternity had not Jesus firmly reminded them of their responsibilities. Having seen His deity, having seen Moses and Elijah ministering to Him, having heard God's own voice validate His Son's ministry, they needed to draw sustenance from the revelation while withholding their testimony until after the resurrection.

I sometimes wonder if Peter, James, and John fully understood, at this point, the tremendous burden of responsibility that had been thrust upon them as leaders of leaders—or if that realization dawned gradually. The men of Jesus' inner circle had been greatly blessed and would be greatly tried. They would know great successes and great failures, exult with great joy and grieve with great sorrow; and in the process they would exemplify for us the great graciousness of our God, who gives us no more than we can bear and fully equips us for every good deed.[1]

A Lesson from Failure
(Matthew 17:14–21; Mark 9:14–29; Luke 9:37–43)

As the Transfiguration witnesses descended the mountain with Jesus, they were met by a large crowd milling around the other disciples. One of the men in the crowd had come looking for Jesus. Upon finding Him absent, he had desperately appealed to the disciples to heal his demon-possessed son. Try as they might, they had been unable to do so.

Now the thoroughly distraught father appealed to Jesus to do something, "if You can." Jesus assured him that "all things are possible to him who believes," to which the father responded, "I do believe; help my unbelief" (Mark 9:22–24). Jesus honored the man's recognition of his dependence on God for the very ability to believe and healed his son. He then turned to His chagrined disciples and used their failure to teach them the necessity of prayer in the life of God's servants. The mustard seed quality of effective faith requires the quickening power of intense communion with God. Those who reap the fruits of ministry are those who sow their seed in prayer.

Notes

1. If you need *great encouragement* in this area, memorize and meditate upon 1 Corinthians 10:13, 2 Timothy 3:16–17, and 2 Corinthians 9:8.

Exercises

Review

1. On the map in appendix C, locate and mark Tyre, Sidon, and Caesarea Philippi. If you have time, investigate a few commentaries and see if you can identify and locate the "Mount of Transfiguration."

2. Relate Paul's words in 2 Corinthians 2:14–16 to Jesus' ministry as the "Bread of Life." How do these words relate to our ministry?

3. Explain the support found in John 6 for the doctrines of election, irresistible grace, and the perseverance (or preservation) of the saints. What implications can you draw from this passage supporting the doctrine of human depravity?

4. How does Jesus' interaction with the Samaritan woman and the Syro-Phoenician woman demonstrate the scope of the gospel message?

5. Describe the critical issues Jesus emphasized with His disciples in this lesson.

6. What did Jesus' disciples learn from the Transfiguration and their failure to heal the demon-possessed boy? (Hint: Different disciples may have learned different things.)

Application

1. Have you ever wanted to walk away from Christianity, "chunk" your faith, and give up on ministry? If so, describe the events that precipitated these desires. What parallels do you see between your situation and the situation described in John 6? Can you identify with Peter's statement, "To whom shall we go?" (v. 68). If so, explain. Explain why genuine Christians *cannot* walk away from their faith, no matter how badly they may think they want to.

2. Can you think of any modern-day examples of what might be called "Corban Christianity"—that is, using the forms of religion to escape responsibility? If so, describe them. Are any of your examples a particular temptation for you personally? If so, how will you resist them?

Digging Deeper

1. Many Christians use Jesus' words in John 6:37, "And the one who comes to Me I will certainly not cast out," in their attempts to refute the biblical doctrine of election. Research this passage thoroughly (in context), and explain the fallacy of this argument.

2. Explain the implications of 2 Corinthians 2:14–16 for evangelism.

Primary Passages

Matthew 8:19–22; 17:22–19:2

Mark 9:38–40

Luke 9:51–10:42

John 7:1–10:21

Supplementary Passages

Mark 9:30–37, 41–10:1

Luke 9:44–50

Before reading the lesson material, please read the primary Scripture passages listed above and as many of the supplementary passages as time allows. Then briefly summarize in your notebook what you have read. (Do not go into detail. Limit your summary to whom the passages discuss, what is being discussed, and where and when the events in the passages occur.)

8

The Light of
the World

Darkness always yields to light
unless the eyes themselves are dark.
Turning on a light
never helps a blind man see.
Jesus was light in a dark world
inhabited by blind men.
They could not see His light
unless He restored their sight as well.
It takes a miracle to open blind eyes.
Those who experience it marvel
at God's glory revealed in
the Light of the World.

Picture, if you will, a shadowy room eerily illumined by the pale glow of an open refrigerator. Behind the refrigerator door cowers a terrified woman, staring fixedly at a barely distinguishable man moving menacingly toward her. As you watch in helpless horror, your mind cries, "Why doesn't she close the door!" Then you remember—the woman is blind. She doesn't close the door because she can't see the light, let alone the towel her pursuer used to keep the door open.

Do you recognize this scene? It's the bone-chilling climax to one of my favorite movies, *Wait Until Dark*. I'm no movie analyst, but I think that scene works so well because of its stunning contrasts: the shadowy room set against the bright refrigerator light; an "underdog" heroine seemingly at the mercy of a powerful attacker; her desperate grasp on the very thing that is giving her away; and her blind inability to act in her own best interests.

The Scripture passages in this lesson intrigue me because they contain some of those same contrasts. We will see in them a dark world illumined by a solitary light glowing in Israel, an "underdog" hero locked in mortal conflict with powerful enemies, religious leaders clinging tenaciously to the means of their own destruction, and people too blind to act in their own best interests. See if you can spot them as we proceed.

Blinded by the Light
(Matthew 17:22–18:35; Mark 9:30–50; Luke 9:44–50)

If anyone has ever suddenly directed a flashlight into your eyes, you know what it means to be "blinded by the light." The pupil of your eye cannot adjust quickly enough to handle a sudden increase in illumination. Instead of the light enabling you to see, it momentarily blinds you.

Jesus' revelation of the startling ramifications of His incarnation, coming so soon after Peter's confession and the Transfiguration, appears to have had exactly that affect on the apostles. Their minds simply could not adjust quickly enough to understand His words, "The Son of Man is going to be delivered into the hands of men; and they will kill Him, and He will be raised on the third day" (Matthew 17:22–23).

Temporarily blinded by the light of such startling truth, the disciples continued resolutely down the dangerous path of their own political aspirations. Jesus, keenly aware of their need to refocus, patiently pursued them with more and more light.

Acknowledging Peter's pivotal leadership position, He reinforced his confession with a faith-solidifying miracle. When Peter mentioned the necessity of paying the two-drachma temple tax, Jesus reminded him of His own inherent exemption from this tax based on His standing as the Son of God, but also of the need to avoid offense. He then sent him to the sea to pick up their tax money from the mouth of a generous fish.

Turning His attention to the group as a whole, Jesus shifted their focus away from earthly greatness to childlike humility. As leaders in His kingdom, they must cultivate servanthood by eliminating stumbling blocks, despising exclusivity, correcting each other in love, and forgiving as they had been forgiven.

Jesus' words speak to us as clearly as they did to the disciples. Those who are chosen by God to accomplish His purposes are frequently blinded by the light of His glorious revelation. How stubbornly we persist in our misguided pursuits when we insist upon walking without His assistance. Only by humbly submitting to the leading of His Spirit can we be assured of serving Him effectively.

Singleness of Eye
(Matthew 8:19–22; 19:1–2; Mark 10:1; Luke 9:51–62; John 7:1–10)

The phrase "singleness of eye" reminds me of working with the microscopes in my high school biology lab. You had to close one eye tightly and place the other one squarely over the eyepiece to study what was trapped on the slide. In that position, you were definitely focused. With all other distractions eliminated from your field of vision, you could concentrate solely on those squirmy little microbes.

When Jesus "resolutely set His face to go to Jerusalem" (Luke 9:51), He did the same thing. He walked intently, refusing to be distracted by inhospitable Samaritans, overzealous disciples, half-hearted followers, and spiteful family members. When James and John asked permission to "command fire to come down from heaven and consume" a haughty Samaritan village (v. 54), they were reminded of His mission. "The Son of Man did not come to destroy men's lives, but to save them" (v. 56). Dealing with the Samaritans was a needless distraction.

When three would-be followers offered excuses for delay, they were summarily rejected. "Allow the dead to bury their own dead," He told one (v. 60). To another He said that no one should look back "after putting his hand to the plow" (v. 62). Their creative excuses were a diverting distraction. When His own brothers encouraged Him to do the "right" thing (go to Jerusalem) for the wrong reason (to seek publicity), they were rebuked. Their bad advice was a prideful distraction.

His time was drawing near and demanded full focus. In the days ahead, Jesus would be characterized by singleness of eye. His concentration on the cross would be complete as He narrowed His ministry to God-ordained essentials.

The Light at the Feast[1]
(John 7:11–8:59)

The Feast of Tabernacles in Jerusalem drew Jews from throughout the land to commemorate God's miraculous dealing with their fathers during the wilderness wanderings. One of the highlights of the feast was the brilliant illumination of the temple in celebration of God's unfailing presence with them. Tragically on this particular occasion, many temple-goers were too blind to see God's actual presence walking among them as Jesus, *the Light of the World,* taught in their midst.

The leaders once again tried to undermine Him, and Jesus responded by asserting that His teaching came from God, while theirs was a perversion of truth. His boldness stirred up controversy among the people. Some insisted that He could not be the Messiah because "we know where this man is from" (John 7:27). Others declared, "When the Christ shall come, He will not perform more signs than those which this man has, will He?" (v. 31). The Pharisees, concerned about the uproar, sent officials to seize Jesus, only to have them return empty-handed, proclaiming to their superiors, "No man ever spoke like this Man!" (v. 46 NKJV).

What had they heard that stopped them in their tracks? An intriguing description of the blind and the sighted. "I am the light of the world; he who follows Me shall not walk in the darkness, but shall have the light of life" (John 8:12). Jesus would soon return to the One who sent Him. Many would seek Him but in their blindness would be unable to find Him. Those with eyes to see, however, would come to Him for satisfaction of their thirst for righteousness and would follow Him as blessed dispensers of "living water," pouring out to others what they had received.

The Pharisees, upon hearing these words, renewed their efforts to discredit His claims, little realizing that they were providing Him another perfect opportunity to assert His deity. Their first assault was a legal one—the Pharisees reminded Him that testimony in one's own defense did not constitute truth in Jewish law, and therefore He should not be believed. Jesus shot back that *His* testimony *was* truth because of who He was, and that He also had the testimony of the Father who sent Him. These two absolutely credible witnesses provided evidence that would stand up in any Jewish court.

"Where is Your Father?" the Pharisees smugly responded (v. 19), unwittingly releasing a flurry of messianic teaching:

> If you knew Me, you would know My Father also. . . . I am not of this world. . . . unless you believe that I am He, you shall die in your sins. . . . He who sent me is true; and the things which I heard from Him, these I speak to the world. . . . When you lift up the Son of Man, then you will know that I am He, and I do nothing on My own initiative, but I speak these things as the Father taught Me. And He who sent Me is with Me; He has not left Me alone, for I always do the things that are pleasing to Him. (vv. 19, 23–24, 26, 28–29)

Emphasizing their blind inability to see God's truth, Jesus condemned them in their sins. Their desire to kill Him invalidated their claim to be sons of Abraham and revealed them to be sons of the Devil instead. "He who is of God hears the words of God; for this reason you do not hear them, because you are not of God" (v. 47). The Pharisees, clutching desperately at their shredded self-respect, accused Jesus of being a demon-possessed Samaritan who claimed superiority over Abraham. Jesus seized the moment to announce, "Before Abraham was born, I am" (v. 58), asserting not only His superiority over Abraham, but His equality with God.

The Pharisees got the point, and picked up stones to throw at Him. But Jesus once again passed through their midst unscathed.

A Blind Man Sees
(John 9:1–10:21)

Since many Jews believed that physical afflictions were caused by sin, we should not be surprised to hear Jesus' disciples ask, "Rabbi, who sinned, this man or his parents, that he should be born blind?" (John 9:2). I am sure *they* were surprised, however, by His answer. "Neither. . . . It was in order that the works of God might be displayed in him. We must work the works of Him who sent Me, as long as it is day; night is coming, when no man can work. While I am in the world, I am the light of the world" (vv. 3–5).

Jesus, the master teacher, used their short-sighted question to broaden their perspective. "Look beyond the suffering to God's ultimate purpose for it," He seems to be saying. God had ordained this man's blindness to provide Jesus with a perfect opportunity to display His identity as the *Light of the World*. What better way to do that than by restoring the physical sight of one who would, in the process, receive spiritual sight as well. Jesus' words also carry a sense of urgency, exhorting His disciples to forego fruit-less theological discussions and pursue essential matters.

Jesus exemplified His teaching by immediately "getting down to business"—the business of displaying the works of God. He applied spittle-moistened clay to the blind man's eyes and commanded him to wash at the Pool of Siloam. The resultant miracle generated much discussion among the man's neighbors, who took him to the Pharisees for a definitive explanation. Characteristically, the Pharisees were baffled. The man's increasing boldness in the face of their escalating desperation is almost comical, and his ultimate excommunication from the synagogue reflects no sin on his part, but the Pharisees' utter frustration with Jesus. The miracle could not be explained away, Jesus' authority could not be undermined, and their backs were against the wall.

When Jesus heard about the excommunication, He sought out the man to deal with his soul. Revealing His identity and calling for belief, Jesus performed an even greater miracle by opening the man's spiritual eyes. Jesus summed up the purpose of His actions by announcing, "For judgment I came into this world, that those who do not see may see; and that those who see may become blind" (v. 39). Only those whose eyes have been opened to their own blindness will inherit eternal life. Those, like the Pharisees, who blindly affirm their ability to see will die in their sin.

Jesus continued to antagonize the Pharisees by comparing their treatment of the man born blind to the action of thieves and robbers who climb surreptitiously into a sheepfold to harm the sheep. The Good Shepherd, on the other hand, enters boldly by the door. The sheep hear His voice and follow Him because their eyes have been opened to know Him.

His condemnation of the Pharisees in this Good Shepherd discourse (John 10:1–21) also provides great comfort to the elect as it describes Jesus' loving relationship with those who know Him. He is the "door" through whom we enter into salvation (v. 9). There in the lush pastures of abundant life, we are joined by sheep from every tribe and nation to rest assured in the protection and care of the One who lays down His life for the sheep.

Corrective Lenses
(Luke 10:1–42)

Even though Christians are no longer blind, their sight may not always be twenty-twenty. Luke devotes chapter 10 of his gospel to describing a few Christians whose vision was much improved when Jesus took the time to fit them with corrective lenses.

A group of seventy followers who were dispatched on a mission very similar to that of the Twelve returned greatly impressed that "even the demons are subject to us in Your name" (v. 17). Jesus corrected their vision by telling them, "Do not rejoice in this, that the spirits are subject to you, but rejoice that your names are recorded in heaven" (v. 20).

A lawyer had to have his glasses adjusted before He could see "who is my neighbor" (v. 29), and Martha needed her bifocals strengthened to see clearly that "only a few things are necessary" (v. 42).

Corrective lenses are nothing to be ashamed of. I wear mine

gratefully—both my physical ones and my spiritual ones. Corrective lenses are a manifestation of the Good Shepherd's great love for the sheep as He does whatever is needed to help us see God's truth clearly. As our vision sharpens under His care, we can rejoice with the disciples to hear His words of affirmation, "Blessed are the eyes which see the things you see [even with corrective lenses], for I say to you, that many prophets and kings wished to see the things which you see, and did not see them" (vv. 23–24).

Notes

1. John 7:53–8:11 is a "problem passage" because most reputable scholars believe it is a scribal insertion rather than part of John's original gospel. It does not appear in the earliest manuscripts and breaks the continuity of the passage as a whole. Rather than go into issues of textual criticism, I have chosen to skip over this section and refer students to reliable commentators for more information on this passage of Scripture.

Exercises

Review

1. On the map in appendix C, review the location of Galilee, Samaria, Judea, Capernaum, and Jerusalem. Also identify the "regions beyond the Jordan." If you have a detailed map of Jerusalem and its environs, locate the temple and the Mount of Olives.

2. Give at least one *specific* example from this lesson of the following contrasts:

   a dark world illumined by a solitary light glowing in Israel:
   an "underdog" hero locked in mortal conflict with powerful enemies:
   religious leaders clinging tenaciously to the means of their own destruction:
   people too blind to act in their own best interests:

Can you think of any modern examples of these contrasts? If so, describe them.

3. Explain in your own words why Jesus' disciples failed to understand His clear statement of the purpose for His incarnation.

4. Reread John 7:1–10:21 and record each of Jesus' references to Himself as "light." Now record each time He refers to "blindness" and to "sight" or the "ability to see." Study each passage you have recorded and explain the point Jesus is making in each case. (Remember to consider the context of each passage, and feel free to consult reliable commentaries if necessary.)

5. Every once in a while I hear someone say, "Jesus never claimed to be God." Reread John 8 and answer this person using information found in that passage. (Remember to give an answer that explains your hope in Christ, is gentle and reverent, and will put to shame those who revile your good behavior in Christ [1 Peter 3:15–17].)

6. Reread Luke 10 and thoroughly explain how "being fitted with corrective lenses" helped the seventy, the lawyer, and Martha see God's truth more clearly. (Hint: Indicate what they could not see before but could see afterward.)

Application

1. Some people *actively* serve God and some *actively* serve Satan, but most people seem *actively* to serve themselves. Describe someone you know who actively serves God. Include elements of his or her character and behavior that indicate active service to God. If you know someone who actively serves Satan, describe that person in the same way. Now describe someone you know who seems to actively serve himself. In which category would you place yourself? Explain. Do you believe it is possible to actively serve yourself without also serving God or serving Satan? Explain.

2. Using the Christians in Luke 10 as possible examples, describe a time in your life when your spiritual vision needed correcting. How did Jesus do this for you? What were you able to see differently as a result of His work in your life?

Digging Deeper

1. Using an exhaustive concordance, Bible encyclopedia, and other reliable study tools, research the primary Jewish feasts: Passover, Pentecost, and Tabernacles. Describe the institution and purpose of each feast, and then explain (1) how each feast pointed toward Christ and (2) how Christ's death and resurrection affected the need to celebrate these feasts.

Primary Passages

Luke 11:1–17:10
John 10:22–11:57

Supplementary Passages

None

Before reading the lesson material, please read the primary Scripture passages listed above and as many of the supplementary passages as time allows. Then briefly summarize in your notebook what you have read. (Do not go into detail. Limit your summary to whom the passages discuss, what is being discussed, and where and when the events in the passages occur.)

9

Much Is Given and
Much Is Required

God is the giver of all good gifts.
In His great love He pours out blessing
on the just and the unjust.
Not all appreciate the gifts He bestows.
Some deny their goodness.
Some deny their Source.
Some deny their purpose.
But all who receive His gifts
will one day give an account,
for great gifts bring great responsibility.
Much is given and much is required.

I am writing this lesson on New Year's Day, 1998, fresh on the heels of completing my New Year's resolutions.

Yes, I still do that—even though my list doesn't seem to change much from year to year. I consistently resolve to eat better, exercise regularly, read more books, and watch less television. But this year, under conviction by the Holy Spirit, I have made one startling new resolution: *to use my time wisely.*

I say "startling" because I make *very good use* of my time now. I rise early, work hard, and get a lot done. However, I have learned from researching this lesson that making very good use of my time doesn't always equate with using it wisely.

Luke and John have taught me that using my time wisely involves using it exclusively to carry out God's plans and purposes for me, and that as a Christian, I am *required* to use it wisely. Why? Because it is part of the "much" that God has given me.

Much is required of me because I have been given *much*. The people we meet in this lesson were also given much by God, and much was required of them in return. As we study together, pay particular attention to the contrast between the way Jesus' disciples and His enemies responded to the "much" God had given them.[1]

Imitate or Deprecate?
(Luke 11:1–54)

Much of the "much" His disciples and enemies had been given was the living example of Jesus Christ. And much of the "much" required of them was imitation of His example. In Luke 11, Jesus encouraged His disciples for doing that but condemned His enemies for doing the opposite.

"Lord, teach us to pray," the disciples requested after watching Him pray (v. 1). Jesus responded with a review of the model prayer He had already taught them and a parable illustrating the importance of persistence in prayer. "Ask . . . seek . . . knock," He tells them (v. 9). "And confidently expect good gifts from your heavenly Father" (my paraphrase).

His enemies, however, insisted upon deprecating Jesus' example by aligning Him with Satan and demanding "a sign from heaven" (v. 16). Jesus denounced their unrighteous motives with righteous reason, explaining the impossibility of a "house divided" continuing to stand (v. 17), and refusing to provide any sign but the "sign of Jonah" (v. 29).

Jesus challenged them to examine the "lamp" of their bodies to see if it was dark, and He compared them to slovenly dishwashers who clean the outside of a cup while leaving the inside filthy. He pronounced "woes" (scathing denunciations tinged with sorrow) upon the leaders for their religious pretensions, haughty behavior, irresponsible teaching, unloving leadership, and over-all wickedness.

God had given them much with which to lead His people and required a great deal from them in return. But instead of fulfilling their responsibilities, they had "taken away the key of knowledge" from the people, refused to "enter in" to the kingdom of God themselves, and hindered "those who were entering in" (v. 52).

Tragically, His words fell on deaf ears. Luke tells us that "the scribes and Pharisees began to be very hostile and to question Him closely on many subjects, plotting against Him, to catch Him in something He might say" (vv. 53–54).

Woeful Warnings
(Luke 12:1–13:35)

The hypocrisy of the Pharisees drew more than condemnation from the Savior. It also sparked an intense clarification of God's revealed truth and a terse warning against their human errors. In Luke 12 and 13, Jesus explained the grandeur of God's gifts and the magnitude of His requirements.

He begins and ends His discourse with the analogy of leaven. His first sentence warns against the "leaven of the Pharisees, which is hypocrisy" (Luke 12:1), and His closing parable compares the kingdom of God to "leaven, which a woman took and hid in three pecks of meal, until it was all leavened" (Luke 13:21). Why the same analogy for two things so completely opposite? Because of the way leaven works. Although it remains visibly hidden in its host, its presence is dramatically revealed when it begins to work. The presence of both the Pharisees and the kingdom of God in the world would have exactly this kind of impact. Jesus explained it this way: "There is nothing covered up that will not be revealed, and hidden that will not be known" (Luke 12:2).

Pharisaic hypocrisy and divine truth were both "hidden" in the world, influencing people in profound but incompatible ways. Each would demand a *choice* of allegiance from those they touched. Their inherent exclusivity eliminated the option of accepting a little of both.

Jesus called His followers to denounce the leaven of the Pharisees and receive the leaven of the kingdom of God. They must not fear those who could kill their bodies, but fear instead the One who "after He has killed has authority to cast into hell" (v. 5). They must confess Christ before men, depending on the Holy Spirit for the appropriate words and resting in Christ's confession of them before the Father.

"Confessing" Christ must not be considered a means of accomplishing worldly purposes. One man who asked Jesus to settle an inheritance dispute drew a rebuke instead, punctuated by a parable describing the tragic fate of a worldly minded man who viewed God's blessing of wealth primarily as a storage problem.

Christ's followers were instructed to disavow the world's preoccupation with worry, recognizing that their heavenly Father would abundantly meet all their needs as they committed their resources to His service. They must also alertly resist the complacency that would erode their effectiveness and leave them startled and ashamed at His unannounced Second Coming.

Peter's question, "Lord, are You addressing this parable to us, or to everyone else as well?" (v. 41), drew a challenging response. *Every* follower of Christ must rightly divide the Word, but influential leaders bore an even heavier responsibility. "From everyone who has been given much shall much be required; and to whom they entrusted much, of him they will ask all the more" (v. 48).

Ironically, following the Prince of Peace would not bring peace on earth, but division. It would divide households and sever friendships. It would kindle an unquenchable fire that would purify some and destroy others. It would, in effect, increase the world's blindness by shining the light of God's glory directly into its eyes.

Jesus then underscored His teaching by responding with a call for repentance to a report about "the Galileans, whose blood Pilate had mingled with their sacrifices" (13:1); emphasizing the limits of God's patience, with a parable of an unproductive fig tree; and challenging hypocritical traditionalism, with yet another Sabbath day healing.

Jesus didn't enjoy pronouncing "woes" upon His enemies. Scripture tells us He grieved over the hardheartedness of those who should have been most receptive to Him. He pleaded with them to "strive to enter by the narrow door; for many, I tell you, will seek to enter and will not be able"—a warning that pious religiosity couldn't open heaven's door (Luke 13:24). The tragedy of their wasted heritage would intensify as they watched many "from east and west and from north and south . . . recline at the table in the kingdom of God" (v. 29), while they were "cast out" (v. 28).

Jesus' grief is portrayed most poignantly as He laments over the city of Jerusalem: "O Jerusalem, Jerusalem, the city that kills the prophets and stones those sent to her! How often I wanted to gather your children together, just as a hen gathers her brood under her wings, and you would not have it!" (v. 34).

The Feast of Dedication
(John 10:22–42)
The Jewish leaders further demonstrated their disregard of all God had given them at the Feast of Dedication in Jerusalem. Stubbornly ignoring obvious evidence, they deviously prodded Jesus toward self-incrimination. "How long will You keep us in suspense? If You are the Christ, tell us plainly" (v. 24).

Jesus replied plainly enough to provoke an attempted stoning. He confronted them with their own irresponsibility. "I told you, and you do not believe; the works that I do in My Father's name, these bear witness of Me. But you do not believe, because you are not of My sheep" (vv. 25–26). Only those chosen by God as His own would recognize the Shepherd He had sent. These particular religious leaders had not been chosen and, therefore, could not see the truth.

Jesus went on to affirm His identity by describing His role in God's extension of grace to the elect. "My sheep hear My voice, and I know them, and they follow Me; and I give eternal life to them, and they shall never perish; and no one shall snatch them out of My hand. My Father, who has given them to Me, is greater than all; and no one is able to snatch them out of the Father's hand. I and the Father are one" (vv. 27–30).

Jesus supported His verbal claims by pointing to His works and the testimony of their own law. He was not guilty of blasphemy because He was telling the truth. The evidence was incontrovertible. The furious Jews again tried to seize Him, but Jesus eluded them. Journeying "beyond the Jordan" where John the Baptist had preached (v. 40), He received "many who believed in Him there" and who were saying, "Everything John said about this man was true" (vv. 41–42).

Emphasizing Requirements
(Luke 14:1–35)

As we read the account of Jesus' dining in the house of a Pharisee where "they were watching Him closely" (v. 1), we can reasonably conclude that the man with dropsy was placed before Him deliberately. Jesus recognized the situation as a "setup" and met it head-on: "Is it lawful to heal on the Sabbath, or not?" (v. 3). After healing the man and sending him away, Jesus, again through parables, condemned the Pharisees' failure to understand and comply with God's requirements.

The parable of the wedding feast highlights their sinful desire for self-exaltation, and the parable of the great supper illustrates their scorning of their privileged standing before God. The chosen nation of Israel had been given much, but had neglected God's great blessings to pursue trivialities. Their callousness had cost them dearly, as the "much" they had been given was withdrawn from them and given to others.

Jesus then challenged the multitudes to "count the cost" of following Him. His call to discipleship is a call to service, not to self-indulgence. God's gracious gift of salvation does not free us to do whatever we want; it empowers us to do what He created us for. We too have been given much, and much is required of us in return.

Contrasts in Teaching
(Luke 15:1–17:10)

Jesus was a master teacher who adapted His instruction to the needs of His hearers. Luke highlights this contrast in the parables contained in chapters 15–17. The parables of the lost sheep, coin, and son, as well as the parable of the rich man and Lazarus, were addressed to Pharisees who spurned the responsibilities associated with all God had given them in favor of self-exaltation. In these parables, Jesus described God's love for His children and condemned the Pharisees for failing to follow His example. By placing religious appearances above the work of God, they revealed the true condition of their hearts.

The remainder of Jesus' teaching, addressed to the disciples, encouraged their transformed willingness to fulfill God's requirements by exhorting them to exercise wisdom in the pursuit of God's kingdom, guard against becoming stumbling blocks to others, and maintain an attitude of humility in their service.

The Raising of Lazarus
(John 11:1–46)

Martha, Mary, and Lazarus were three of Jesus' closest earthly friends. So when Lazarus fell gravely ill, his sisters immediately sent for Him. However, instead of rushing to the dying man's bedside, Jesus delayed two full days before announcing, "Let us go to Judea again" (v. 7).

The disciples tried to dissuade Him from going with reminders of recent attempts on His life. Jesus' response stressed a transcendent necessity: "Are there not twelve hours in the day? If anyone walks in the day, he does not stumble, because he sees the light of this world. . . . Lazarus is dead, and I am glad for your sakes that I was not there, so that you may believe; but let us go to him" (vv. 9, 14–15). Thomas, remembered for his doubts, certainly expressed none here when he urged his fellow disciples, "Let us also go, that we may die with Him" (v. 16).

By the time they arrived in Bethany, Lazarus had been dead four days. Martha and Mary both greeted Jesus with faithful words tinged with disappointment and grief: "Lord, if You had been here, my brother would not have died" (vv. 21, 32). Jesus engaged Martha in a prolonged discussion, culminating in a call for her to respond to Him as God incarnate: "I am the resurrection and the life; he who believes in Me shall live even if He dies, and everyone who lives and believes in Me shall never die. Do you believe this?" (vv. 25–26). Her answer was as sure and certain as Peter's in a similar situation: "Yes, Lord; I have believed that You are the Christ, the Son of God, even He who comes into the world" (v. 27).

Jesus' spectacular miracle on this occasion established His identity beyond reasonable doubt. The love of God incarnate was revealed as He wept with sinful people over the wages of their sin, and the power of His Word was revealed as He called Lazarus forth from the grave.

Those who watched Lazarus "come forth" found neutrality impossible. John reports that "many therefore of the Jews, who had come to Mary and beheld what he had done, believed in Him. But some of them went away to the Pharisees, and told them the things which Jesus had done" (vv. 45–46).

The Withdrawal to Ephraim
(John 11:47–57)

The Pharisees, upon hearing about this latest miracle, convened a council to discuss their options. None doubted the veracity of the report, and all were concerned for their political futures. He had to be stopped.

Caiaphas, the high priest, fueled their bloodlust even as he prophetically proclaimed the fulfillment of Jesus' messianic mission: "You know nothing at all, nor do you take into account that it is expedient for you that one man should die for the people, and that the whole nation should not perish" (vv. 49–50).

The council took Caiaphas's words to heart, and "from that day on they planned together to kill Him" (v. 53). Jesus withdrew to the city of Ephraim to remain in seclusion with His disciples. As Passover approached, people swarmed into Jerusalem buzzing with excitement. The Pharisees had ordered that anyone who knew Jesus' whereabouts must report it so that they could seize Him.

Would He come for the Feast? And if He did, what would happen to Him? If the Pharisees succeeded in killing Him, what would happen to His followers? Could they be expected to remain faithful to a dead man?

Yes, they could. From those who had been given much, much could be required.

Notes

1. Much of the material in this portion of Luke's gospel repeats Jesus' teachings in the Sermon on the Mount. This should not surprise us since Jesus was a master teacher who knew the value of repetition.

Exercises

Review

1. On the map in appendix C, locate and mark Perea, Bethany, and Ephraim.

2. Describe the "much" that God had given each of the following. Describe also what was required of them because of what they had been given. How did each respond to God's requirements?

   Jesus' disciples:
   the Pharisees:
   the multitudes who followed Jesus:
   Mary, Martha, and Lazarus

3. State in one or two sentences (your own words, please) the main point of each of the following parables. Since all of these were not covered in detail in the lesson, feel free to consult reliable commentaries if necessary.

   the persistent friend (Luke 11:5–8):
   the rich fool (Luke 12:16–21):
   the watchful slaves (Luke 12:35–40):
   the faithful steward (Luke 12:42–48):
   the unproductive fig tree (Luke 13:6–9):

the wedding feast (Luke 14:8–11):
the great supper (Luke 14:16–24):
the lost sheep, lost coin, and lost son (Luke 15:4–32):
the unrighteous steward (Luke 16:1–13):
the rich man and Lazarus (Luke 16:19–31):

Which of these parables were addressed to the Pharisees and which to Jesus' disciples? Why did Jesus teach different parables to different audiences?

4. Reread Luke 11:37–54 and list the "woes" Jesus pronounced against the Pharisees along with a brief explanation of each.

5. Explain why Jesus used the analogy of leaven to describe the influence of the Pharisees *and* the kingdom of God upon the world.

6. Reread John 10:22–11:57 and describe the ways Jesus asserted His deity in these verses.

Application
1. Give some specific examples of the "much" you have been given by God. Then describe (specifically, please) what is required of you in view of what you have been given. How well are you fulfilling those requirements? Explain. What specific changes do you need to make in order to better fulfill them? How will you implement these needed changes?

2. Using examples from your own life, explain why the idea that much is required from those to whom much has been given emphasizes *God's grace*—not our works. (Hint: Is God's grace about what *we don't have to do* or is it about what *God equips and enables us to do?*)

Digging Deeper
1. James Montgomery Boice, in his commentary on John, says that John 10:22–30 contains the most highly condensed state-

ments of the doctrine of grace in all of Scripture. He explains that these verses teach that (1) people in themselves are unable to believe in Jesus Christ for salvation, (2) those who believe do so because God acts in grace to elect them into the company of His people, (3) all whom God elects will believe, and (4) none of those who believe are ever lost. Study these verses in context and explain how this passage supports Dr. Boice's statements. What insights have you gained into the doctrine of grace from your study of this passage in light of Dr. Boice's statements?

Primary Passages

Matthew 19:3–20:16;
    21:12–22
Mark 10:32–11:26
Luke 17:11–18:17; 19:1–27
John 12:1–11

Supplementary Passages

Matthew 20:17–21:11
Mark 10:1–31
Luke 18:18–43; 19:28–48
John 12:12–19
Zechariah 9:9

Before reading the lesson material, please read the primary Scripture passages listed above and as many of the supplementary passages as time allows. Then briefly summarize in your notebook what you have read. (Do not go into detail. Limit your summary to whom the passages discuss, what is being discussed, and where and when the events in the passages occur.)

10

Exalted Through Humility

Jesus came not to be served but to serve,
and to give His life a ransom for many.
He taught His followers to please the Father
by imitating His example,
which none found easy to do.
Their bent on exalting themselves
clashed with the Father's design
to have them
exalted through humility.

Ask any group of children or young people, "What do you want to be when you grow up?" and you will receive a number of interesting responses. Astronauts, doctors, nurses, teachers, lawyers, engineers, presidents, truck drivers, mommies, and daddies make frequent appearances on youngsters' "most wanted" list. However, one worthy occupation rarely gets mentioned. Think for a moment. Have you ever heard a child or young person say, "When I grow up, I want to be a slave"?

Why is that? Think again for a moment. Those first yearnings after particular occupations reveal our innate human desire for *importance*. All of us long to be noticed, to stand out from the crowd, to make a contribution, to be exalted above the masses in some way. And yet Scripture reveals God's desire for each of us to be a slave.

Jesus, who patterned for us a life absolutely pleasing to God, told His disciples He had come, not to be served, but to serve. The apostle Paul, whose life was also worthy of imitation, repeatedly described himself as a "bondslave"—one whose life is completely under the control of another. Romans 6:18 describes Christians as "slaves of righteousness," and verse 22 describes the benefits accruing to those who are "enslaved to God."

Why does God call us to slavery? Because that is the only call that makes sense. *He* is righteous, holy, and sovereign. *We* are sinful, depraved, and dependent. All of *His* purposes will be accomplished (Isaiah 46:10), and *we* cannot resist His will (Romans 9:19) or straighten what He has bent (Ecclesiastes 7:13). We were created to glorify Him and enjoy Him forever—and we can only do that as His slaves.

We don't have to fear this servitude, however. There is no better career choice than "slave of God." The job description is challenging, the benefits are outstanding, and the retirement package can't be beat. You don't need any special training, and you can't bring your own tools. He will teach you everything you need to know and fully equip you to do His work. Because the selection process is *gracious,* only the completely unqualified need apply. Those who are chosen will receive, free of charge, all of the faith, repentance, and humility needed to accept the position.

The apostle James summarized the requirements and rewards of slavery to God when he said, "But He gives a greater grace. Therefore it says, 'God is opposed to the proud, but gives grace to the humble.' Submit therefore to God. . . . Humble yourselves in the presence of the Lord, and He will exalt you." (4:6–7, 10)

The people we will meet in this lesson learned the necessity of being *exalted through humility.* Most of them had a difficult time understanding that truth, just as you and I do today, but God was (and is) faithful. Jesus taught them by word and example that the only way to achieve the satisfaction of *righteous* exaltation is by humbly submitting, as slaves, to God.

A Look at Humble, Submissive Slaves
(Luke 17:11–18:14)

Luke illustrates the nature of God's humbly submissive slaves in his account of Jesus' interaction with a group of lepers, a group of Pharisees, and His own disciples somewhere "on the way to Jerusalem . . . between Samaria and Galilee" (Luke 17:11).

The lepers stood at a safe distance and begged Him for healing. When He replied, "Go and show yourselves to the priests" (v. 14), they eagerly obeyed and were healed as they went. Only one, however, turned back to say thanks. Jesus' question "Were there not ten cleansed? But the nine—where are they?" highlights a key characteristic of humble, submissive slaves (v. 17). They glorify God by joyfully expressing their gratitude for His magnificent blessings.

In answer to some Pharisees who wanted to know "when the kingdom of God was coming," He said that it was not coming with "signs to be observed" but was already in their midst (vv. 20–21). They couldn't see it because of their arrogant aversion to slavery.

The disciples, on the other hand, were blessed with an explanation of the glorious nature of God's kingdom. The kingdom was present among them in the person of Jesus Christ Himself and would eventually reside in each of them in the person of the Holy Spirit. Their presence in the world would testify of God's grace and glory and leave sinful humanity without excuse at the culmination of the kingdom when Christ returns to claim His own.

Jesus told His disciples that humble, submissive slaves of God would be characterized by their preoccupation with eternal matters. They would, therefore, not be caught off guard when the kingdom comes "as the lightning, when it flashes out of one part of the sky . . . on the day that the Son of Man is revealed" (vv. 24, 30).

He continued by describing (in parable) God's slaves as persistent prayer warriors whose unflagging confidence in God's promise of provision also brings Him great glory. And He concluded with another parable highlighting the difference between righteous slaves and self-righteous hypocrites. "I tell you," He said, ". . . everyone who exalts himself shall be humbled, but he who humbles himself shall be exalted" (Luke 18:14).

The Selflessness of Slaves
(Matthew 19:3–20:16; Mark 10:1–31; Luke 18:15–30)

Jesus used a Pharisaic question, a visit from some children, and an inquiry from a rich young man to teach His disciples about the *selflessness* of God's slaves. His answer to the Pharisees' question "Is it lawful for a man to divorce his wife for any cause at all?" (Matthew 19:3) sparked a comment from the disciples that revealed their need for teaching on this subject. After hearing Jesus review God's standards for marriage, they said to Him, "If the relationship of the man with his wife is like this, it is better not to marry" (v. 10). Jesus confronted them with the self-centeredness of their thinking by reminding them that the choice of singleness should be motivated by physical necessity or ministry commitment, not by the difficulty of adhering to God's creation ordinances.

He addressed their self-centeredness again when they rebuked some parents who were bringing their children to Jesus for blessing. "Let the children alone," He said, "and do not hinder them from coming to Me; for the kingdom of heaven belongs to such as these" (v. 14).

Knowing full well the importance and difficulty of this lesson, Jesus returned to it once more after His encounter with a rich young man. As He watched him walk away grieving over the necessity of complete commitment, Jesus said to His disciples, "It is easier for a camel to go through the eye of a needle, than for a rich man to enter the kingdom of God. . . . With men this is impossible, but with God all things are possible" (vv. 24, 26).

The disciples' response revealed the progress they had made as well as the distance they still had to go. "Behold, we have left everything and followed You; what then will there be for us?" (v. 27). Jesus lovingly reassured them of the rewards awaiting them in heaven but cautioned them with the enigmatic statement, "But many who are first will be last, and the last, first" (v. 30).

He illustrated that statement with a parable emphasizing a landowner's right to reward his workers in accordance with his own standard of generosity. Jesus was exposing the disciples' *self-centered* tendency to exalt their "selfless" service above that of others and to expect a proportionate reward from God. The parable not only depicts the righteousness of God's reward system but encourages them selflessly to regard the joy of service as part of its own reward.

Slow Learners
(Matthew 20:17–28; Mark 10:32–45; Luke 18:31–34)

Jesus' disciples, like so many of us today, were notoriously slow learners. But (praise God!) Jesus was a remarkably patient teacher. As they continued on the road to Jerusalem, He warned them about what to expect when they got there. "Behold, we are going up to Jerusalem; and the Son of Man will be delivered to the chief priests and scribes, and they will condemn Him to death, and will deliver Him to the Gentiles to mock and scourge and crucify Him, and on the third day He will be raised up" (Matthew 20:18–19).

Amazingly, even such pointed teaching failed to penetrate their rock-hard–headedness. Luke tells us, "And they understood none of these things, and this saying was hidden from them, and they did not comprehend the things that were said" (Luke 18:34). Characteristically, their lack of understanding was quickly revealed in their actions.

James and John, obviously still wrestling with the ramifications of His "last shall be first, and the first last" statement, approached Him with a request for prominent positions in the kingdom. Jesus responded with gentle correction rather than the blunt rebuke they deserved—and with even greater gentleness when the other ten disciples "became indignant" with them (Matthew 20:24).

He reminded them that God's design was servant-leadership, not lordly rule. "Whoever wishes to become great among you shall be your servant, and whoever wishes to be first among you shall be your slave; just as the Son of Man did not come to be served, but to serve, and to give His life a ransom for many" (vv. 26–28).

Joyful Slaves in Jericho
(Matthew 20:29–34; Mark 10:46–52; Luke 18:35–19:27)

Not everyone Jesus encountered was a slow learner, however. Jericho was home to at least two decidedly quick studies. A blind beggar named Bartimaeus was sitting by the road as Jesus entered the city, heard the commotion, and cried out repeatedly, "Jesus, Son of David, have mercy on me!" (Mark 10:47). "Son of David" was a title used by Jews to refer to their expected Messiah and one that, significantly, Jesus readily accepted.

When so addressed, He stopped, called the man to Himself, and asked him what he wanted. Bartimaeus apparently knew who Jesus was and fully expected to be healed. Matthew and Mark both indicate that he *left his cloak* (a necessary and cherished possession) when he went to Jesus, obviously confident that he would be able to retrieve it once his sight had been restored.

Once inside the city, Jesus quickly recognized another gifted student perched in the branches of a handy Sycamore tree. Zaccheus, the local tax collector, was too short to see over the crowd and too despicable to be given a front-row seat, but too determined to give up. Climbing that tree did little for his dignity but did wonders for his soul. The Savior spotted him and said, "Zaccheus, hurry and come down, for today I must stay at your house" (Luke 19:5).

I can almost see the ecstatic little man scrambling and tumbling out of those branches in his eagerness to become a slave. What a startling conversion! No arguments, no excuses, no counter-proposals—just a joyful willingness to do all (and more) that was asked of him.

Jesus then capitalized on the living example of Zaccheus by teaching a parable regarding the importance of using God's gifts profitably in the kingdom. Not everyone is given the same type or amount of gifts, but everyone shares the responsibility to be productive. "I tell you," Jesus concluded, "that to everyone who has shall more be given, but from the one who does not have, even what he does have shall be taken away" (v. 26).

Misunderstood Slaves
(John 12:1–11)
Before reaching Jerusalem, Jesus stopped in Bethany to dine with His dear friends, Mary, Martha, and Lazarus. The events of the dinner teach us about misunderstood slaves of God—misunderstood *genuine* slaves, and misunderstood *false* ones.

Mary was a genuine slave of God whose favorite position was sitting at Jesus' feet. On this occasion, her sensitive nature responded to the nearness of His death with a lavish display of devotion that was misunderstood by those around her. As she broke open the pound of costly "perfume of pure nard" (v. 3) and anointed Jesus' feet, astonished gasps must have filled the house as quickly as did the powerful fragrance. Surely many were thinking what Judas actually said: "Why was this perfume not sold for three hundred denarii, and given to poor people?" (v. 5).

Only those who shared Mary's devotion to her Master could have understood and rejoiced in her passion for worship. Jesus exonerated her gesture with a rebuke to her critics. "Let her alone, in order that she may keep it for the day of My burial. For the poor you always have with you, but you do not always have Me" (vv. 7–8).

Another "slave of God" was also misunderstood that day—the false slave, Judas Iscariot. Judas's "slavery" was motivated by the greed common to those who align themselves with Christ for selfish reasons. John, writing with the benefit of hindsight, explains that Judas's question was not nearly as fiscally responsible as it appeared on the surface: "Now he said this, not because he was concerned about the poor, but because he was a thief, and as he had the money box, he used to pilfer what was put into it" (v. 6).

Approaching the Apex of History
(Matthew 21:1–22; Mark 11:1–26; Luke 19:28–48; John 12:12–19)

Those slaves of God who have studied human history from an eternal perspective place its fulcrum in the tiny land of Israel during the life of Christ. It's not a large fulcrum upon which to balance so much history. The base is no more than thirty-three years wide, while the apex narrows to the few agonizing hours Jesus spent on the cross. But because history's fulcrum is "the human episode in the divine life," it does its job perfectly.

Even though every element in the life of Christ is critically important to human history, those surrounding the apex take on an unusual intensity. As Jesus "approached Jerusalem, at Bethphage and Bethany, near the Mount of Olives"(Mark 11:1), His death was less than a week away. The events of those final days grip us so vigorously because they transpired in the shadow of the cross.

Jesus' persistent teaching of *exaltation through humility* would now be enhanced by the impact of His personal example.

He entered Jerusalem triumphantly, but humbly, on the back of a donkey, pausing to weep out His grief over the fate of the city:

> If you had known in this day, even you, the things which make for peace! But now they have been hidden from your eyes. For the days shall come upon you when your enemies will throw up a bank before you, and surround you, and hem you in on every side, and will level you to the ground and your children within you, and they will not leave in you one stone upon another, because you did not recognize the time of your visitation. (Luke 19:42–44)

His second cleansing of the temple demonstrated one of humility's surprising qualities—an appropriate (when necessary) fierceness in carrying out God's will. Humble, submissive slaves of God are not always calm, quiet, and composed. They have been known to turn the world upside down—in more ways than one! It's no wonder Mark tells us, "The chief priests and the scribes . . . began seeking how to destroy Him; for they were afraid of Him, for all the multitude was astonished at His teaching" (11:18).

His cursing of the fig tree offers us a vivid illustration of self-exaltation's eventual end. The profusion of foliage masking the tree's barrenness was pretension personified—but no match for the Master. One look within unmasked its hypocrisy.

Those who persist in exalting themselves will surely share the fig tree's fate. But those slaves of God who humble themselves under His mighty hand will, by that same hand, surely be exalted at the proper time.

Exercises

Review

1. Explain why God calls Christians to slavery. In your explanation, be sure to include why slavery is the only call that makes sense and how this call relates to being exalted through humility.

2. Reread Luke 17:11–18:14 and describe at least three characteristics of humble, submissive slaves of God found in these
   verses.

3. Reread Matthew 19:3–20:16 and describe the disciples' need
   for teaching on the subject of selflessness. How did Jesus meet
   their need?

4. Compare and contrast the "slow learners" who followed Jesus
   and the "quick studies" who lived in Jericho.

5. Describe how the actions of Mary and the words of Judas at
   the dinner in Bethany were both misunderstood by others.

6. Explain the lesson to be learned from the withered fig tree.

Application

1. List some specific examples of your own desires for importance. For example, what kinds of things do you say and do
   that reveal your longing to be noticed, to stand out from the
   crowd, or to make a contribution to the world? Do your desires for importance reflect a tendency to exalt yourself or to
   glorify God? Explain. What specific changes do you need to
   make in your thinking, attitudes, and behavior in order to
   more consistently glorify God rather than exalt yourself? How
   will you accomplish these changes?

2. Of the people mentioned in this lesson—the disciples, the ungrateful lepers, the grateful leper, the Pharisees, Bartimaeus,
   Zaccheus, and Mary—which one do you identify with most,
   and why?

Digging Deeper

1. Explain how the life of Christ can be viewed as the fulcrum
   of human history.

Primary Passages
Matthew 21:23–25:46

Mark 12:41–44

John 12:20–50

Supplementary Passages
Mark 11:27–12:40; 13:1–37

Luke 20:1–21:38

Before reading the lesson material, please read the primary Scripture passages listed above and as many of the supplementary passages as time allows. Then briefly summarize in your notebook what you have read. (Do not go into detail. Limit your summary to whom the passages discuss, what is being discussed, and where and when the events in the passages occur.)

LESSON

11
God's Greatest Commandment

Pharisees, Sadducees,
scribes, Herodians, lawyers—
they knew God's law,
bound it on their hands,
wore it on their foreheads,
and wrote it on their doorposts.
The mighty words of the Shema
were constantly on their lips,
but never in their hearts.
"Love the Lord your God
with all your heart,
and with all your soul,
and with all your mind"—
God's greatest commandment.

"Love" may well be the most overused and abused word in the English language. We *love* our parents, our spouses, and our children—and we *love* green chili enchiladas. We *love* rare antiques, classic cars, and fine art—and we *love* a good mystery novel. We *love* football games, quilting bees, and bridge tournaments—and we *love* God.

Popular music assures us that "love is a wonderful thing," and "what the world needs now is love, sweet, love." But the classical philosopher Plato didn't agree. He warned his students that "love is a grave mental disease."[1]

Abigail Van Buren, of "Dear Abby" fame, says that love and money are a lot alike in that "they're both wonderful as long as they last."[2] George Bernard Shaw quips, "There is no sincerer love than the love of food."[3] And then there's this gem of porcine wisdom from Miss Piggy: "When you are in love with someone, you want to be near him all the time, except when you are out buying things and charging them to him."[4]

Obviously the little word "love" covers a lot of ground in English usage. It describes deep-seated emotional ties between life-long companions, as well as casual sexual encounters between relative strangers. It expresses friendship, loyalty, and fidelity, as well as incidental preferences, changing tastes, and passing fancies. It communicates complete seriousness, profound depth, and touching pathos, as well as lighthearted jest, flippant irrelevancy, and crudeness. What a busy—and remarkably imprecise—little word!

Jesus, however, used the little word very differently than we do. His comments about love recorded in the Bible are extremely precise—although somewhat disturbing to our fallen minds. Love, He says, is a *commandment*—God's greatest commandment.

We tend to recoil from the very idea. How can *love* be commanded? It can be because it is God's love Jesus is talking about, not human love. God's love is not something we "fall into," but something we purposefully will to do. It is not characterized by emotion so much as it is by activity. The love Jesus talked about can be defined as self-sacrificial action motivated by a God-given desire to meet the needs of others in response to His commands recorded in Scripture.

God commands us to love this way because this is the way He loves us (1 John 4:7–21). God's love for us is no giddy emotion. It is motivated by our need for reconciliation with Him—and by His willful intent to meet that need at great cost to Himself. When we reflect His love in the way we love, we glorify Him and enjoy the benefits He bestows only upon the faithful.

As Jesus' ministry drew closer to its climax, the contrast sharpened between those who should have understood God's love but didn't and those who had no apparent reason to understand it but did. As we study through this lesson together, pay particular attention to this widening gulf between Jesus' followers and His enemies.

The Last Word
(Matthew 21:23–22:46; Mark 11:27–12:37; Luke 20:1–44)

Common threats have been known to forge unlikely alliances. Even bitter enemies temporarily suspend hostilities when expediency demands joining forces against a common foe. Such was the case with Jesus' enemies. The Pharisees, Sadducees, and Herodians had always kept pretty busy squabbling with each other, but saw in Jesus a good reason to kiss and make up. If He were not stopped, they would all be destroyed. Little did they realize, however, that even their united effort would prove no match for the Son of God.

Their first assault came in the form of yet another challenge to His authority. Confronting Him in the temple, representatives from the Sanhedrin asked, "By what authority are You doing these things, and who gave You this authority?" (Matthew 21:23). He countered with a question of His own, worded so skillfully that they couldn't answer it without undermining their own authority. "We do not know," they hemmed (v. 27), igniting a series of three censorious parables exposing their lack of love for God.

In the first, Jesus aligned them with the hypocritical son of a landowner who promised to work in the family vineyard but failed to do so. Their similar lack of love for the Father, revealed in their refusal to believe John's testimony about Jesus, would keep them out of the kingdom while the "tax gatherers and harlots" (v. 32), who did heed John's message, would be granted free entry.

The second parable expanded on the first. A landowner planted a vineyard, rented it out to tenant-farmers, and left town. When harvest time came, he sent his servants and his own son to collect his profits. All were beaten, stoned, and killed by the tenants. "Therefore," Jesus said, "when the owner of the vineyard comes, what will he do to those vine-growers?" (v. 40). His listeners wit-lessly drew the noose tighter around their own necks by an-swering, "He will bring those wretches to a wretched end, and will rent out the vineyard to other vine-growers, who will pay him the proceeds at the proper seasons" (v. 41).

Does this sound familiar? Remember King David's discussion with Nathan about a little ewe lamb? (If not, read 2 Samuel 12:1–15.) Jesus' response to these Sanhedrin emissaries is but a longer version of Nathan's "You are the man!" Because they had rejected God's hand-crafted cornerstone, the kingdom of God would be ripped from their grasp and given to those who would produce the fruit of it.

The third parable erased all possible doubts as to Jesus' con-demnatory intent. It concerned a wedding feast given by a king for his son to which the invited guests refused to come. The en-raged king destroyed those ungrateful subjects and graciously be-stowed their spurned privilege upon others.

Bloodied but unbowed, the Jewish leaders retreated and "coun-seled together how they might trap Him in what He said" (Matthew 22:15). A coalition of Pharisees and Herodians fired off a devious question concerning the poll-tax that was quickly parried by a marvelous answer. And a delegation of Sadducees fared no bet-ter with an extreme scenario ridiculing the afterlife. So the ever-confident Pharisees gave it one last shot. Gathering around Him, they pushed a well-coached lawyer forward to ask, "Teacher, which is the great commandment in the Law?" (v. 36).

Jesus' reply, His final word to them, pinpointed the reason for their alienation from God and clarified the issue of His own au-thority for all time: " 'You shall love the Lord your God with all your heart, and with all your soul, and with all your mind,' " He said. "This is the great and foremost commandment. The second is like it, 'You shall love your neighbor as yourself.' On these two com-mandments depend the whole Law and the Prophets" (vv. 37–40).

His words exposed the utter fallacy of their self-righteousness. They were trusting in their own works—their law-keeping—to earn favor with God. However, their works were motivated, not by love for God, but by desire for self-exaltation. Keeping the law, Jesus told them, rests upon loving God and loving neighbors, and they loved only themselves. They didn't love God; they had rejected His Son. And they didn't love their neighbors; they exploited them. Their lack of love prevented them from keeping the law and left them trusting in their works to no avail.

"What do you think about the Christ," He asked them. "Whose son is He?" (v. 42). Their answer, "The son of David," sparked His application of Psalm 110:1 to Himself. He was their Messiah, the Christ, the son of David. Had they fulfilled the law by loving God, they would have recognized and acknowledged Him. Because they didn't, they stood condemned.

Seven Woes and a Blessing
(Matthew 23:1–39; Mark 12:38–44; Luke 20:45–21:4)

Jesus then turned His attention to His followers and warned them, in graphic detail, of their leaders' loveless hypocrisy. He did so by upholding the authority of their position while challenging the unrighteousness of their practice. "The scribes and the Pharisees have seated themselves in the chair of Moses; therefore all that they tell you, do and observe, but do not do according to their deeds; for they say things, and do not do them" (Matthew 23:2–3).

Their position as religious leaders made their evil practices all the more reprehensible as they burdened others with loads they themselves refused to carry and sought glory from men rather than from God. How deserving they were of the woes Jesus pronounced against them.

> Woe to you, scribes and Pharisees, hypocrites, because you shut off the kingdom of heaven from men. . . .
>
> Woe to you, scribes and Pharisees, hypocrites, because you devour widows' houses, even while for a pretense you make long prayers. . . .
>
> Woe to you, scribes and Pharisees, hypocrites, because you travel about . . . to make one proselyte . . . twice as much a son of hell as yourselves.
>
> Woe to you, blind guides . . .
>
> Woe to you, scribes and Pharisees, hypocrites! For you tithe mint and dill and cummin, and have neglected the

weightier provisions of the law: justice and mercy and faithfulness. . . .

Woe to you, scribes and Pharisees, hypocrites! For you clean the outside of the cup and of the dish, but inside they are full of robbery and self-indulgence. . . .

Woe to you, scribes and Pharisees, hypocrites! For you . . . outwardly appear righteous to men, but inwardly you are full of hypocrisy and lawlessness.

Woe to you, scribes and Pharisees, hypocrites! For . . . upon you may fall the guilt of all the righteous blood shed on earth. (vv. 13–35)

The indictment, falling from the lips of the incarnate Christ, was damning. Their lovelessness reflected the hardhearted depravity that would separate them from God for all eternity.

In stark contrast to the loveless activities of the Jewish leaders stands the loving action of one poor widow. Jesus watched from the shadows as she entered the temple and dropped two small copper coins in the offering box. No fanfare, no desire to be seen of men, no thought of self-exaltation—only complete and willing surrender of everything she had to the One who created and sustained her.

Jesus endears her to our memory with words blessing the love that marked her out as a true child of God. "Truly I say to you, this poor widow put in more than all the contributors to the treasury; for they all put in out of their surplus, but she, out of her poverty, put in all she owned, all she had to live on" (Mark 12:43–44).

From the Few to the Many
(John 12:20–50)
The visit of some Greeks, following so soon after Jesus' condemnation of the Jewish leaders, seems to mark a significant shift in the Messiah's ministry focus. Up to this point, He has concentrated upon the "lost sheep of the house of Israel," but now, at the hour of His glorification, His language becomes all-inclusive. "If *anyone* serves Me, let him follow Me; and where I am there shall My

servant also be; if *anyone* serves Me, the Father will honor him" (v. 26).

The loving heart of God incarnate had held salvation's door open as long as possible to recalcitrant Israel, but she had stubbornly refused to enter. Now, as Jesus prepared to be "lifted up from the earth" (v. 32), He announced His death would draw *all men* to Himself.

His final gospel message was directed to a Gentile audience: "For a little while longer the light is among you. Walk while you have the light, that darkness may not overtake you; he who walks in the darkness does not know where he goes. While you have the light, believe in the light, in order that you may become sons of light" (vv. 35–36).

And His final assessment of Israel's condition concerned their fulfillment of Isaiah's prophecy of their apostasy. "Lord, who has believed our report? And to whom has the arm of the Lord been revealed? . . . He has blinded their eyes, and He hardened their heart; lest they see with their eyes, and perceive with their heart, and be converted, and I heal them" (vv. 38, 40).

Jesus summarized His impact on Jew and Gentile alike by affirming that whoever believed in Him believed in God, and whoever rejected Him rejected God. Every person's ultimate destiny rests upon his or her response to the One who has come as light into the world to speak, not on His own initiative, but at the Father's command.

The Olivet Discourse
(Matthew 24–25; Mark 13:1–37; Luke 21:5–38)

Jesus capitalized on His disciples' casual reference to the "wonderful buildings" (Mark 13:1) of the temple complex to draw their attention to future events. "Do you not see all these things? Truly I say to you, not one stone here shall be left upon another, which will not be torn down" (Matthew 24:2). A little later, at their request, He elaborated in what has become known in the church as the Olivet discourse.

He began by warning them not to be misled about the sign of His coming and the end of the age. Many will come claiming to be the Christ, there will be wars and rumors of wars, famines, and earthquakes. Jesus described these as the beginning of birth pains and prepared His disciples for persecution. It will be a time of great apostasy, lawlessness, and lovelessness, but those who persevere to the end will prove themselves elect of God, holy and beloved. He also described a time of tribulation—a reference to the destruction of Jerusalem in A.D. 70 and perhaps also to the events immediately preceding His Second Coming.

The emphasis of His message was preparedness. Be alert, He said. No one knows the hour of His return, and only the foolish will be caught off guard. Parables concerning a fig tree, faithful and evil servants, ten virgins, and a group of stewards underscore this emphasis.

He then reiterated the core of the gospel message. At the end of the age when the Son of Man comes in His glory, the sheep who heard His voice and followed Him will be separated from the goats who refused to listen. The sheep will be invited to inherit the kingdom prepared for them from before the foundation of the world, while the goats will be cast into the eternal fire prepared for the Devil and his angels.

And what will be the distinguishing characteristic separating the sheep from the goats? Love. God's love. The sheep will be the ones who fed the hungry, clothed the naked, and visited the prisoners. They will be the ones who did these things self-sacrificially, in response to God's command rather than to be seen of men.

"Truly," He will say to them, "to the extent that you did it to one of these brothers of Mine, even the least of them, you did it to Me" (Matthew 25:40).

Notes

1. Robert Byrne, *The 1911 Best Things Anybody Ever Said* (New York: Fawcett Columbine, 1986), 31.

2. Carolyn Warner, *The Last Word: A Treasury of Women's Quotes* (Englewood Cliffs, N.J.: Prentice Hall, 1992), 207.

3. Byrne, *The 1911 Best Things,* 326.

4. Ibid., 284.

Exercises

Review

1. Explain how Jesus can command us to love.

2. In one or two sentences, state the main point of each of the following parables:

   the obedient and disobedient sons (Matthew 21:27–32):
   the traveling landowner (Matthew 21:33–44):
   the king's wedding feast (Matthew 22:2–14):
   the fig tree (Matthew 24:32–33):
   the faithful and evil slaves (Matthew 24:45–51):
   the ten virgins (Matthew 25:1–13):
   the stewards' talents (Matthew 25:14–30):

3. Explain how understanding God's greatest commandment exposes the fallacy of self-righteousness.

4. List the seven "woes" Jesus pronounced against the Jewish leaders, and try to give a specific example of why they deserved each one.

5. How did the focus of Jesus' ministry seem to change in John 12:20–50?

6. Summarize the main points of Jesus' Olivet discourse. How does His teaching about the separation of the sheep from the goats illustrate His statement of God's greatest commandment?

Application

1. Read 1 John 4:7–21 thoughtfully and prayerfully. From these verses, describe (as fully as you can) how God has loved you.

   Now, based on these verses, describe how you are to love God and others. List specific actions you can take to love God and others the way you should. (Remember to answer the questions: Who? What? When? Where? and How?) What changes do you need to make in your thinking, attitudes, and behavior to perform these actions?

2. It has been said that the essence of all sin is a lack of love for God. List several sins you have committed recently, and explain how each reflects a lack of love for God. Now list some specific acts of love toward God that will help you overcome sins like these in the future.

Digging Deeper

1. Reread John 12:42–43 and consider the following question: Were these rulers truly converted to Christian faith? Study the tenth chapter of Romans in relation to this issue, along with any other pertinent passages you may discover, and write out your answer to this question. Then discuss your conclusions with your pastor, one of your elders, or another spiritual leader in your church.

Primary Passages

Mark 14:1–52

John 13–17

Supplementary Passages

Matthew 26:1–56

Luke 22:1–53

John 18:1–12

Before reading the lesson material, please read the primary Scripture passages listed above and as many of the supplementary passages as time allows. Then briefly summarize in your notebook what you have read. (Do not go into detail. Limit your summary to whom the passages discuss, what is being discussed, and where and when the events in the passages occur.)

12

Passover Is Fulfilled!

The darkest night in Egypt was when the firstborn died.
But blood on Jewish doorposts told the angel, "Pass them by."
Passover was a remembrance of that fateful night.
Not meant to be forever, it pointed to the Light.
The death of God's own Son brought deliverance to His own,
not from human bondage but from enslavement to our sin.
Never again would they eat it the way they did until
the Light had come to conquer death.
Passover is fulfilled!

The first Passover meal was eaten on a horrific night. Egypt was reeling from nine ghastly plagues that couldn't possibly get worse but then suddenly did. The hours before midnight had been eerily quiet, but at that precise moment, the first mother screamed. Her cries were soon echoed by countless others as the night filled up with wailing. Every Egyptian mother's firstborn child was dead.

But the Hebrews' children had escaped. Their parents had followed God's order and smeared lamb's blood on their doors. The angel of death, following his own specific order, saw the blood and passed them by. The blood of the lamb had saved them then, and the blood of the Lamb still saves us today.

The first Passover meal was not to be forgotten. God instituted a celebration of remembrance as a picture of deliverance. It looked back to deliverance from bondage in Egypt and forward to deliverance from bondage to sin. The lamb that was slain as meat for the dinner portrayed the Lamb that was slain as atonement for sin.

The last Passover meal was also eaten on a horrific night. The disciples were reeling from the ghastly reality of inescapable revelation and would give way to their fears before morning had dawned. They would fail their Master by scattering like sheep, denying His name, and hiding in shame. But the Master would not fail them. He would struggle and sweat and cry out to God. But He knew why He had come and would fulfill God's plan.

The last Passover meal was not to be forgotten either. Christ instituted a new celebration to make sure it was not. As we begin looking at the closing events in the life of our Lord, pay particular attention to how Jesus saw His imminent death and resurrection as a fulfillment of the Jewish Passover celebration.

Prediction and Betrayal[1]
(Matthew 26:1–16; Mark 14:1–11; Luke 22:1–6)

As Jerusalem prepared for Passover, the vast majority of its bulging populace scurried about completely oblivious to the eternal drama playing out around them. Jesus had alerted His disciples, forcefully and inescapably, of the part He would play: "You know that after two days the Passover is coming, and the Son of Man is to be delivered up for crucifixion" (Matthew 26:2). And the chief priests and the elders gathered with the high priest, Caiaphas, to fine-tune the plot. They would seize Him by stealth and put Him to death, but "not during the festival, lest a riot occur among the people" (v. 4).

Judas, the traitorous villain, received his cue by satanic indwelling and hurried away to the Jewish leaders with an offer of betrayal. It didn't take long to seal the diabolical bargain, and Judas returned to those he had spurned to watch for a "good opportunity to betray" the ultimate Passover Lamb (v. 16).

The Passover Meal
(Matthew 26:17–35; Mark 14:12–31; Luke 22:7–38; John 13:1–14:31)

The Passover celebration was actually a week-long affair officially designated as the Feast of Unleavened Bread. On the first day of the Feast, the Passover lamb was sacrificed and the memorial meal was eaten. Thus we find in the Gospel accounts Jesus' disciples coming to Him on the "first day of Unleavened Bread" and asking, "Where do you want us to go and prepare for you to eat the Passover?" (Mark 14:12).

He sent Peter and John into town to find a man carrying a pitcher of water (an unusual activity for a man in those days) who had a room "furnished and ready" for them to use (v. 15). I can't help but wonder what they were thinking as they prepared the room for their last meal together, but the Gospel writers reveal a still-selfish focus that was far from the Lord.

Another dispute about relative greatness and a stubborn resistance to humbly serving others prompted Jesus to teach them a lesson. Rising from supper and girding Himself as the lowliest of slaves, He proceeded to wash their filthy feet. His exhortation to follow His example reinforced His consistent emphasis upon servant leadership. "For I gave you an example that you also should do as I did to you. Truly, truly, I say to you, a slave is not greater than his master; neither is one who is sent greater than the one who sent him. If you know these things, you are blessed if you do them" (John 13:15–17).

Having finally secured their undivided attention, He proceeded to define the eternal significance of the meal they were eating. Identifying the bread as His body broken for them and the wine as a new covenant in His blood poured out for them, He declared His fulfillment of the Passover sacrifice. "I have earnestly desired to eat this Passover with you before I suffer; for I say to you, I shall never again eat it until it is fulfilled in the kingdom of God" (Luke 22:15–16).

He then identified and dispatched the traitor among them to set in motion God's preordained plan, and informed the others that they too would desert Him that night. His declaration of betrayal and desertion prompted protestations of loyalty from an over-confident Peter: "Lord, with You I am ready to go both to prison and to death!" (v. 33).

"I say to you, Peter," the Lord responded, "the cock will not crow today until you have denied three times that you know Me" (v. 34). Peter, shocked and appalled, was not left without hope. The Lord also assured Him that even though Satan had been granted permission to sift him like wheat, Jesus had prayed that his faith would not fail. "When once you have turned again," He admonished this pivotal leader, "strengthen your brothers" (v. 32).

He then comforted Peter in particular and the disciples in general with assurances regarding His heavenly preparation for their eventual reunion.

> Let not your heart be troubled; believe in God, believe also in Me. In My Father's house are many dwelling places; if it were not so, I would have told you; for I go to prepare a place for you. And if I go and prepare a place for you, I will come again, and receive you to Myself; that where I am, there you may be also. And you know the way where I am going. (John 14:1–4)

During the question and answer session that followed, Jesus laid the groundwork for His fulfillment of Passover. To Thomas's "How do we know the way?" He described the exclusivity of God's plan of redemption: "I am the way, and the truth, and the life; no one comes to the Father, but through Me" (vv. 5–6). To Philip's request to see the Father, He responded, "He who has seen Me has seen the Father. . . . I am in the Father, and the Father is in Me" (vv. 8–10). And to Judas (not Iscariot) who asked why He was disclosing Himself to them and not to the world, He explained the blessings of loving obedience.

Because He had come into the world as God incarnate to satisfy God's wrath against human sin once and for all, the elect of God stood redeemed and reconciled. They would glorify the Father by praying in Jesus' name and receiving their requests. They would testify of God's greatness in the power of the Holy Spirit as they obeyed His commands and preached His truth. And they would demonstrate God's sovereign care as overcomers, living above fear and trouble while resting in His peace.

The hour of His death was fast approaching, but the comfort of His words would sustain them. The "ruler of the world" was coming to do what God had granted him permission to do, and he would meet them at Gethsemane. "Arise," Jesus said to them. "Let us go from here" (vv. 30–31).

Teaching on the Way
(John 15:1–16:33)
Jesus reinforced on the way to Gethsemane what He had taught them in the upper room. Abiding in Him as a branch abides in the vine would be necessary for productive kingdom labor, effective prayer, and peaceful overcoming.

Love was the basis for all they would do. Just as Jesus had loved them to the uttermost by laying down His life, they would love those to whom they would minister. They had been chosen by God, elevated as friends of Jesus, and appointed to carry out the work He had begun. Their holiness would shine in a sin-darkened world, illuminating wickedness and generating hatred. "If they persecute Me," Jesus told them, "they will also persecute you. . . . But all these things they will do to you for My name's sake" (vv. 20–21). Because Jesus had come, the world had no excuse for its sin and hated Him for it. As the disciples continued to proclaim His message, the world would hate them for the very same reason.

Jesus spoke, not to discourage them, but to keep them from stumbling. They needed to know what was in store and that God had ordained it. They needed to know that God's Holy Spirit would be with them and that they would not suffer alone or without reason. The Holy Spirit would comfort, guide, teach, and sustain them. He would glorify Christ by bearing witness of Him and disclosing the things of God to them.

Their sorrow would seem overwhelming when He left them, but they would see Him again. They could rest assured in the Father's love because they had loved His Son and believed He came from the Father.

As John 16 draws to a close, I can picture the little band of men gathering around an intense Jesus as He stopped on the path to summarize masterfully all that He'd said during the walk to the garden. "These things I have spoken to you, that in Me you may have peace. In the world you have tribulation, but take courage; I have overcome the world" (v. 33).

Jesus Prays for His Own
(John 17:1–26)

I can picture Jesus then extending His arms so as to encircle His men, lifting His eyes to the Father in heaven, and praying for those He would soon leave behind. "Father," He said. "The hour has come" (v. 1). The work He had covenanted with the Father to do in eternity past was now at hand. He prayed for Himself, asking the Father to glorify Him as He had glorified the Father on earth "having accomplished the work" He had been given to do (v. 4).

He prayed for the men standing with Him that night—men God had selected and given to Him. He had, in turn, given them God's truth, which they had believed. Now He was leaving them alone in the world. He had guarded them thus far but could do so no longer, so He commended them lovingly into His Father's care.

He also prayed for us, amazing as that may sound. "I do not ask in behalf of these alone, but for those also who believe in Me through their word" (v. 20). And He prays for the unity of all believers around the truth of God's Word "that the world may believe that Thou didst send Me" (v. 21).

This beautiful prayer, truly "the Lord's Prayer," highlights the love among the members of the Holy Trinity that has been extended to the elect on earth. What a privilege to be loved with the same love with which God loved the Son! The prayer also sets the pattern for our human relationships. Each believer's divine relationship with the Trinity creates a bond with every other believer that glorifies God's name and testifies of His character in our dark and decaying world.

Jesus Prays for Himself
(Matthew 26:36–46; Mark 14:32–42; Luke 22:39–46; John 18:1)

The real horror of that night played out in the Garden of Gethsemane. The agony of Jesus as He stared sin in the face was beyond all human comprehension. We cannot imagine the agony of One who had never known sin contemplating the prospect of *becoming sin* on our behalf and being separated from the Father in the process.

Separated from the Father? How could He bear it? They were one in essence and nature, but they could not be one in sin-bearing. That He had to do—alone. He had never been alone. And now He had to be alone with sin. That was the horror of Gethsemane.

"My Father," He prayed, "if it is possible, let this cup pass from Me" (Matthew 26:39). Every fiber of His Holy being cried out for some other solution to the problem of sin, but there was none.

"My Father, if this cannot pass away unless I drink it, Thy will be done" (v. 42). The struggle ended in great submission. Sweat drops of blood lay on the ground. An angel, urgently dispatched by a hovering Father, ministered to the beloved Son in whom He was still well pleased. The deed would be done. The deliverance pictured in the Passover would be accomplished.

And where were the disciples at the height of this horror? Sound asleep on the ground, offering not one bit of comfort. He had pleaded three times for their alert support, but the temptation to sleep was too great to resist. They had failed Him this night and would fail Him again. But the strength of His love was greater than all failures combined.

As He shook them awake some time around midnight, He could already hear the expected commotion. "Arise, let us be going; behold, the one who betrays Me is at hand!" (v. 46).

Betrayal and Arrest
(Matthew 26:47–56; Mark 14:43–52; Luke 22:47–53;
John 18:2–12)

Judas had arrived, "accompanied by a great multitude with swords and clubs, from the chief priests and elders of the people" (Matthew 26:47). Identifying Jesus with a kiss, he betrayed Him into the hands of His enemies and consigned his own soul to hell.

Jesus, protective of His flock to the end, gave Himself up but demanded that His disciples be released. Peter, perhaps still too groggy to be thinking (or swinging) straight, grabbed his sword and swiped at the nearest intruder—Malchus, the high priest's slave, who fortunately lost only an ear instead of his head.

"Stop! No more of this" (Luke 22:51). Jesus' command froze the assault. "Put your sword back into its place; for all those who take up the sword shall perish by the sword. Or do you think that I cannot appeal to My Father, and He will at once put at My disposal more than twelve legions of angels?[2] How then shall the Scriptures be fulfilled, that it must happen this way?" (Matthew 26:52–54).

Touching Malchus, He restored the ear, then turned to the mob and quietly declared, "Have you come out with swords and clubs to arrest Me as against a robber? Every day I used to sit in the temple teaching and you did not seize Me. But all this has taken place that the Scriptures of the prophets may be fulfilled" (vv. 55–56).

The Lamb of God, pictured by Passover, was then seized and led away to slaughter while "all the disciples left Him and fled" (v. 56).

Notes

1. Most commentators agree that the synoptic accounts of the anointing of Jesus at the home of Simon the leper in Bethany correspond to the account of John 12:1–8 covered in lesson 11. Therefore, I have not addressed those passages in this lesson.

2. A Roman legion contained six thousand men. Seventy-two thousand angels would have been a match for any mob.

Exercises

Review

1. Compare and contrast the first Passover meal with the last Passover meal.

2. Reread John 13:1-20 and explain why Jesus washed His disciples' feet. Focus on the interaction between Peter and Jesus, and see if you can explain why this encounter was important enough for the Holy Spirit to include in John's gospel.

3. Describe the primary issues Jesus discussed with His disciples at the last Passover meal. Now describe the primary issues He discussed with them on the way to the Garden of Gethsemane. Do you see a relationship between these issues? If so, explain.

4. What did Jesus pray about in John 17? Why is this prayer as important for us today as it was for the disciples then?

5. Describe the "horror of Gethsemane." Reread the Gospel accounts of Gethsemane and describe the interaction between Jesus and His disciples during this time. What does this interaction tell us about Jesus? About the disciples? About ourselves?

6. Describe two or three specific ways Jesus demonstrated God's love during His betrayal and arrest. Now, see if you can describe how the events of this lesson demonstrate His willingness to display God's special love for the elect.

Application

1. Reread John 13:1-16:33 carefully and prayerfully, paying particular attention to what Jesus said about love. Now go back and record His specific teachings about love in these chapters. See if you can outline these teachings in a way that will help you explain them to someone else.

   From your study of this passage, answer the following questions as specifically as you can. What is love? How did Jesus love His disciples (then and now)? How should you love Him? Do you love Him as you should? (Give specific examples.) How can you love Him more effectively this week? (Give specific examples.)

2. Outline "the Lord's Prayer" found in John 17. What does it tell you about love? How does it set the pattern for your behavior in your relationships with others?

Digging Deeper

1. Study John 15:1–6 using any good reference material available to you and answer the following questions as thoroughly as you can. What does the picture of the vine, vinedresser, and branches depict about the relationship between Jesus, the Father, and believers? Who are the branches that do not bear fruit? Who are the branches that do bear fruit? (Pay particular attention to what happens to both kinds of branches.) What is the fruit that is born? If you have time, study the rest of chapters 15 and 16, and explain why this illustration is a good introduction for the material contained there.

2. Should Christians today celebrate Passover? Why or why not? Research this issue thoroughly and discuss your ideas with one or more of your church leaders.

Primary Passages

Matthew 26:57–28:20
Luke 22:63–24:53
John 18:12–14; 19–24;
    19:23–21:25

Supplementary Passages

Mark 14:53–16:20
Luke 22:54–62
John 18:15–18; 25–19:22

Before reading the lesson material, please read the primary Scripture passages listed above and as many of the supplementary passages as time allows. Then briefly summarize in your notebook what you have read. (Do not go into detail. Limit your summary to whom the passages discuss, what is being discussed, and where and when the events in the passages occur.)

13

A Triumph of Grace

Why the cross?
One reason alone.
For the praise of His glory.
A triumph of grace.

Have you ever wondered why God bothered with salvation? He didn't have to, you know. He could have continued living in perfect Trinitarian harmony for all eternity without creating anything or anybody. Nothing in Him needed anything outside of Him for completion, contentment, or enjoyment. He was (and still is) fully self-contained, self-sufficient, and self-satisfied.

So why did He do it? Why breathe His life into a created being who would choose rebellion over obedience? Why choose some of that being's sinful progeny to adopt for His own? Why sacrifice His Son to satisfy His wrath against those He had chosen? Why give us His Spirit as the seal of His promise?

Why did He bother?

The apostle Paul gives us the reason—and repeats it three times to make sure that we get it. God chose us before the foundation of the world to be His holy, blameless, adopted children *to the praise of the glory of His grace* (Ephesians 1:3–6). He sacrificed His Son to secure our inheritance so that we would be *to the praise of His glory* (vv. 11–12). And He gave us His Spirit as the seal of His promise to redeem us, again, *to the praise of His glory* (vv. 13–14).

He bothered with salvation because His own glory was worth it: worth the effort of the Creation; worth the humiliation of the Incarnation; and worth the indignity of the Spirit's indwelling. His glory was worth it, but we certainly weren't. If we alone were the reason, it wouldn't have happened. The reason we benefit from the praise of His glory is because one aspect of His glory is His marvelous *grace.*

The good news of Calvary is its triumph of grace. As we work through this, our final lesson, concentrate on the way the life-changing events surrounding Jesus' crucifixion and resurrection display God's glory, and rejoice in the privilege of joining in His praise.

A Blasphemous Charge of Blasphemy
(Matthew 26:57–68; 27:1–2; Mark 14:53–65; 15:1;
Luke 22:54, 63–23:1; John 18:12–14, 19–24)

The Jews had not wanted to arrest Jesus during the Feast, but God had providentially forced their hand. Now that Jesus was in custody, they decided to act swiftly (albeit illegally) to execute Him as quickly as possible. They took Him first to Annas, the former high priest, who questioned Him carefully but in vain. Jesus refused to answer his unauthorized questions and was rudely bound over to Caiaphas, the ruling high priest.

The unexpected timing of Jesus' arrest sent the chief priests and the council madly scavenging for prosecution witnesses in the middle of the night. And needless to say, they weren't very successful. The only "testimony" they could present before Caiaphas proved so laughably inconsistent that Jesus refused any attempt at defense against it.

Caiaphas, determined to convict in spite of the evidence, jumped into the proceeding with a carefully calculated demand: "I adjure You by the living God, that You tell us whether You are the Christ, the Son of God" (Matthew 26:63).

Jesus' ready response, "You have said it yourself," gave him his grounds (v. 64). Tearing his robes in skillfully feigned grief, the high priest of hypocrisy committed the very sin he attributed to Christ by pronouncing God in the flesh guilty of blasphemy.

As dawn was breaking that Passover morning, the Sanhedrin met to make it official. Jesus must die, but they could not do it. Binding Him again, they hurried to Pilate, the governor, whose Roman authority was needed to validate their death sentence.

The Grief of Two Sinners
(Matthew 26:58, 69–75; 27:3–10; Mark 14:66–72;
Luke 22:54–62; John 18:15–18, 25–27)

As Jesus was being tried in Caiaphas's court, His devoted disciple Peter was also being tried in the courtyard below. Following Jesus at a distance during the evening's events, he had gained entry to the courtyard in the company of a fellow disciple known to the high priest (probably John). Undoubtedly cold and most certainly nervous, he sought the warmth of the fire and the anonymity of the crowd, only to be recognized as one of the prisoner's disciples.

Three times he was challenged, and three times he denied his association with Jesus. The third denial, uttered with an oath, still hung in the air as a cock's crow reverberated through the silent courtyard and Jesus Himself stepped onto the porch. Peter's eyes locked on those of the Savior as he remembered the words spoken only a few hours before: "Before a cock crows today, you will deny Me three times" (Luke 22:61). Unbearable grief born out of love drove him from Jesus in repentant remorse. Peter "went out and wept bitterly" (v. 62).

Not far away, another was grieving in a much different way. Unbearable guilt over his betrayal of innocence drove Judas to return the price of the Lamb. "What is that to us? See to that yourself!" the priests snarled in contempt (Matthew 27:4) as he fled from their presence in self-hating despair. Dashing the coins to the floor of the sanctuary, he ended his life as ineptly as he had lived it. Botching an attempt at suicide by hanging, he fell headlong and "burst open in the middle," leaving as his legacy of depravity the name "Hakeldama" for the "field of blood" where he landed (Acts 1:18–19).

Rome Lends a Hand
(Matthew 27:11–31; Mark 15:1–20; Luke 23:2–26; John 18:28–19:16)

Pilate tried hard not to execute Jesus. He believed the Man was innocent and said so repeatedly. Amazed by Jesus' composure, alarmed by his wife's dream, and fearful of the angry mob, He sought every available avenue of escape.

Twice he tried a change of venue. "Take Him yourselves, and judge Him according to your law," he told the Jewish accusers (John 18:31), assuming the charges were purely religious. The Jews then cleverly charged Jesus with treason, closing off Pilate's first route of escape. Upon questioning them further and discovering Jesus was from Galilee, Pilate sought another exit by sending Him to Herod.

That route proved circular, however, as Herod got nowhere and sent Jesus right back. Pilate then tried reasoning with the Jews: "I have found no guilt in this man regarding the charges which you make against Him. No, nor has Herod, for he sent Him back to us; and behold, nothing deserving death has been done by Him. I will therefore punish Him and release Him" (Luke 23:14–16). But the crowd was unwilling to listen to reason and "cried out all together, saying, 'Away with this man, and release for us Barabbas!' " (v. 18).

"What evil has this man done?" Pilate persisted, still desperately searching for any escape (v. 22). The virulent crowd then turned upon Pilate. "If you release this Man, you are no friend of Caesar" (John 19:12). Pilate knew he was beaten and conceded defeat. Calling for a basin and water, he dramatically washed his hands in front of them, declaring, "I am innocent of this Man's blood; see to that yourselves" (Matthew 27:24). The crowd was quite willing to oblige, venting their rage in reckless self-condemnation: "His blood be on us and on our children!" (v. 25).

The Roman soldiers then stripped Jesus of His garments, dressed Him in a scarlet robe, jammed a crown of thorns upon

His head, mocked Him, and beat Him severely before leading Him away to be crucified.

Death in the Afternoon
(Matthew 27:32–66; Mark 15:21–47; Luke 23:26–56; John 19:17–42)

Jesus was on the verge of collapse when He left Pilate's court and immediately stumbled under the weight of His heavy wooden cross. A passerby named Simon from the land of Cyrene was conscripted into service and carried the cross the rest of the way. Arriving at Golgotha well before noon, they crucified the Lord of Glory between two common thieves.

Pilate had followed them, apparently still trying to assuage his guilt. He wrote an inscription to put on the cross. "Jesus the Nazarene, the King of the Jews" (John 19:19), it declared in Hebrew, Latin, and Greek. The chief priests were incensed and demanded he change it. "Write . . . He said, 'I am King of the Jews' " they insisted (v. 21), but Pilate refused.

The soldiers divided up His garments while spectators and chief priests jeered and mocked: "If you are the Son of God, come down from the cross. . . . He saved others; He cannot save Himself. . . . He trusts in God; let Him deliver Him now" (Matthew 27:40–43). The two thieves joined in the cruel abuse, but one finally repented and was forgiven his sin. "Truly I say to you, today you shall be with Me in Paradise," Jesus told Him (Luke 23:43), extending God's grace to one more of the elect.

A small band of women along with one man stood by in silence, overwhelmed by their grief. Jesus looked down and spotted His mother leaning heavily on the arm of His beloved disciple John, her heart finally pierced through by Simeon's prophesied sword. "Women, behold your son!" He said to the woman, and to the disciple, "Behold your mother!" consigning her gently to John's loving care (John 19:26–27).

At noon the sky darkened, and the horror of Gethsemane played out on the cross. Three hours later, Jesus cried out in anguish, "My God, My God, why hast Thou forsaken Me?" (Matthew 27:46) and dismissed His Spirit, paying in full for the sins of the church. The veil of the temple ripped top to bottom. The earth shook, and rocks split asunder. Graves were opened and once-dead saints walked in the city. A trembling centurion took it all in and summed up the display of God's power in one profound statement: "Truly this was the Son of God!" (v. 54).

Later that evening, the Jews approached Pilate again, suggesting that the legs of the criminals be broken so they could die quickly and be removed from their crosses before Passover began. But since Jesus had already died, His legs were not broken, fulfilling yet another of Scripture's prophecies.

Joseph of Arimathea, a secret disciple, and Nicodemus then came forward to claim the body, preparing it quickly for burial and placing it in a new garden tomb. Following closely behind them, the faithful band of loyal women noted the location of the tomb so that they could return later to complete the burial procedures.

The chief priests and the Pharisees met with Pilate one last time to remind him of Jesus' predictions of His resurrection and suggest that appropriate precautions be taken. "You have a guard; go, make it as secure as you know how," Pilate agreed (v. 65), relieved to believe that the nightmare was over.

He Is Risen! He Is Risen Indeed!
(Matthew 28:1–15; Mark 16:1–13; Luke 24:1–49; John 20:1–31)

No human guard could forestall the fulfillment of Jesus' predictions, however. After the Sabbath, the women returned to the tomb to find the stone rolled away from an empty grave. The waiting angel greeted the women, "Do not be afraid; for I know that you are looking for Jesus who has been crucified. He is not here, for He has risen, just as He said. Come, see the place where He was lying. And go quickly and tell His disciples that He has risen from the dead" (Matthew 28:5–7).

They turned to obey and ran right into Jesus. Falling in worship, they heard Him declare, "Do not be afraid; go and take word to My brethren to leave for Galilee, and there they shall see Me" (v. 10). Wasting no time, they ran to the disciples and gasped out their story. Peter and John ran back to the tomb where they beheld an astounding sight. The grave clothes lay undisturbed but empty—indisputable evidence of the resurrection's reality.

Jesus lingered with them forty more days, ministering to their needs and preparing them for service. Mary Magdalene was comforted, Thomas was convinced, two on the road to Emmaus were instructed, and the disciples were commissioned as foundational leaders of His fledgling church.

He "opened their minds to understand the Scriptures" (Luke 24:45) and impressed upon them the importance of their mission.

> Thus it is written, that the Christ should suffer and rise again from the dead the third day; and that repentance for forgiveness of sins should be proclaimed in His name to all the nations, beginning from Jerusalem. You are witnesses of these things. And behold, I am sending forth the promise of My Father upon you; but you are to stay in the city until you are clothed with power from on high. (vv. 46–49)

One on One with Peter
(John 21:1–25)

Peter, however, needed special attention. His fall had been great and left horrible scars. Jesus, however, knew God's purpose behind it. Exceptional service demands exceptional brokenness, and Peter had been chosen for exceptional service. Jesus met him in Galilee on the shore of the lake. Over a breakfast of fish, they discussed their relationship. "Do you love me, Peter?" Jesus asked him three times, offering a triple rebuttal of Peter's triple denial. Jesus also restored Peter's hope of his predestined inheritance with the words, "Tend my lambs. . . . Shepherd My sheep. . . . Tend My sheep. . . . You follow Me!" (vv. 15–17, 22).

Instructions to All
(Matthew 28:16–20)

Broadening His focus to include the whole group, Jesus proclaimed the scope of God's glorious grace. "All authority has been given to Me in heaven and on earth," He told them. "Go therefore and make disciples of all the nations, baptizing them in the name of the Father and the Son and the Holy Spirit, teaching them to observe all that I commanded you; and lo, I am with you always, even to the end of the age" (vv. 18–20).

What an awesome blessing for them and for us! The triumph of grace extends past our redemption to include transformation. Not only saved, not only secure, but also equipped to serve Him in love. We too play a part in the praise of His glory.

Exercises

Review

1. Describe the trial of Jesus, pointing out why He was brought before both religious *and* civil courts on different charges.

2. Describe Pilate's reluctance to pass sentence on Jesus. What does Pilate's behavior tell you about the way Jesus lived His life on earth?

3. Compare and contrast Peter's denial of Jesus and his declaration of love after the Resurrection. How did Jesus care for Peter during this time of great need?

4. Describe the attitude and behavior of each of the following people (or groups of people) toward Jesus while He hung on the cross:

   Pilate:
   bypassing spectators:
   chief priests:
   the two thieves:
   the women:
   John:
   the trembling centurion:

   To what do you attribute their differing reactions?

5. How did Jesus minister to His followers during the forty days following His resurrection? (Give specific examples.)

6. Based on your study of *God with Us,* explain in your own words why the glory of Calvary is a triumph of grace.

Application

1. Reread Matthew 28:18–20. How does God's grace equip you to obey the commands in these verses? Given your current life situation (single, married, career woman, young mother, grandmother, retired, healthy, ill, struggling, or comfortable), describe some specific ways you can "make disciples." (Remember those questions: Who? What? When? Where? and How?)

2. Take some time to think about your salvation as equipping you through transformation to play a part in the praise of God's glory. How does this aspect of salvation shape your view of the church as a whole and your local church in particular? How does it affect your attitude toward evangelism? Toward Bible study? Toward family, career, and community involvement?

3. Summarize the most significant insights you have gained as a result of studying *God with Us.* How will these insights affect the way you live as a Christian in the world?

Digging Deeper

1. Explain the qualitative difference between Peter's remorse over his sin of denying Jesus and Judas's remorse over his sin of betraying Him. In your explanation, you will want to consider the nature of the two men, the nature of their sins, and the end result of their remorse.

2. Review the Gospel accounts of Jesus' trials, noting when He spoke and when He remained silent, and explain why He spoke when He did and why He remained silent when He did.

APPENDIX A

What Must I Do to Be Saved?

A strange sound drifted through the Philippian jail as midnight approached. The sound of human voices—but not the expected groans of the two men who had earlier been beaten with rods and fastened in stocks. Rather, the peaceful singing of praises to their God.

While the other prisoners quietly listened to them, the jailer dozed off, content with the bizarre calm generated by these two preachers, who, hours before, had stirred up so much commotion in the city.

Suddenly a deafening roar filled the prison as the ground began to shake violently. Sturdy doors convulsed and popped open. Chains snapped and fell at prisoners' feet. Startled into full wakefulness, the jailer stared at the wide-open doors and realized his prisoners' certain escape guaranteed his own impending death. Under Roman law, jailers paid with their lives when prisoners escaped. Resolutely, he drew his sword, thinking it better to die by his own hand than by Roman execution.

"Stop! Don't harm yourself—we are all here!" a voice boomed from the darkened inner cell. The jailer called for lights and was astonished to discover his prisoners standing quietly amid their broken chains. Trembling, he rushed in and fell at the feet of the two preachers. As soon as he was able, he led them out of the prison and asked, "Sirs, what must I do to be saved?"

— — —

In the entire history of the world, no one has ever asked a more important question. The jailer's words that night may well have been motivated by his critical physical need, but the response of Paul and Silas addressed his even more critical spiritual need: "Believe in the Lord Jesus, and you shall be saved, you and your household" (Acts 16:31).[1]

If you have never "believed in the Lord Jesus," your spiritual need, just like the jailer's, is critical. As long as your life is stained with sin, God cannot receive you into His presence. The Bible says that sin has placed a separation between you and God (Isaiah 59:2). It goes on to say that your nature has been so permeated by sin that you no longer have any desire to serve and obey God (Romans 3:10–12); therefore, you are not likely to recognize or care that a separation exists. Your situation is truly desperate because those who are separated from God will spend eternity in hell.

Since sinful hearts are unresponsive to God, the only way sinners can be saved from their desperate situation is for God to take the initiative. And this He has done! Even though all men and women deserve the punishment of hell because of their sin, God's love has prompted Him to save some who will serve Him in obedience. He did this by sending His Son, the Lord Jesus Christ, to remove the barrier of sin between God and His chosen ones (Colossians 2:13–14).

What is there about Jesus that enables Him to do this? First of all, He is God. While He was on earth, He said, "He who has seen Me has seen the Father" (John 14:9), and "I and the Father are one" (John 10:30). Because He said these things, you must conclude one of three things about His true identity: (1) He was a lunatic who believed He was God when He really wasn't; (2) He was a liar who was willing to die a hideous death for what He knew was a lie; or (3) His words are true and He is God.

Lunatics don't live the way Jesus did, and liars don't die the way He did, so if the Bible's account of Jesus' life and words is true, you can be sure He *is* God.

Since Jesus is God, He is perfectly righteous and holy. God's perfect righteousness and holiness demands that sin be punished (Ezekiel 18:4), and Jesus' perfect righteousness and holiness qualified Him to bear the punishment for the sins of those who will be saved (Romans 6:23). Jesus is the only human who never committed a sin; therefore, the punishment He bore when He died on the cross could be accepted by God as satisfaction of His justice in regard to the sins of others.

If someone you love commits a crime and is sentenced to die, you may offer to die in his place. However, if you have also committed crimes worthy of death, your death cannot satisfy the law's demands for your crimes *and* your loved one's. You can only die in his place if you are innocent of any wrongdoing.

Since Jesus lived a perfect life, God's justice could be satisfied by allowing Him to die for the sins of those who will be saved. Because God is perfectly righteous and holy, He could not act in love at the expense of justice. By sending Jesus to die, God demonstrated His love *by acting to satisfy His own justice* (Romans 3:26).

Jesus did more than die, however. He also rose from the dead. By raising Jesus from the dead, God declared that He had accepted Jesus' death in the place of those who will be saved. Because Jesus lives eternally with God, those for whom Jesus died can be assured they will also spend eternity in heaven (John 14:1–3). The separation of sin has been removed!

Ah, but the all-important question remains unanswered: What must *you do* to be saved? If God has sent His Son into the world for sinners, and Jesus Christ has died in their place, what is left for you to do? You must respond in faith to what God has done. This is what Paul meant when he told the jailer, "Believe in the Lord Jesus, and you shall be saved."

Believing in the Lord Jesus demands three responses from you: (1) an understanding of the facts regarding your hopeless sinful condition and God's action to remove the sin barrier that separates you from Him; (2) acceptance of those facts as true and applicable to you; and (3) a willingness to trust and depend upon God to save you from sin. This involves willingly placing yourself under His authority and acknowledging His sovereign right to rule over you.

But, you say, how can I do this if sin has eliminated my ability to know and appreciate God's work on my behalf? Rest assured that if you desire to have the sin barrier that separates you from

God removed, He is already working to change your natural inability to respond. He is extending His gracious offer of salvation to you and will give you the faith to receive it.

If you believe God is working to call you to Himself, read the words He has written to you in the Bible (begin with the book of John in the New Testament) and pray that His Holy Spirit will help you understand what is written there. Continue to read and pray until you are ready to *repent,* that is, to turn away from sin and commit yourself to serving God.

Is there any other way you can be saved? God Himself says no, there is not. The Bible He wrote says that Jesus is the only way the sin barrier between you and God can be removed (John 14:6; Acts 4:12). He is your hope, and He is your *only* hope.

If you have questions or need any help in this matter, please write to The Evangelism Team, Providence Presbyterian Church, P. O. Box 14651, Albuquerque, NM 87191, before the day is over. God has said in His Bible that a day of judgment is coming, and after that day no one will be saved (Acts 17:30–31; 2 Thessalonians 1:7–9). The time to act is now.

Notes

1. See Acts 16:11–40 for the full biblical account of these events.

APPENDIX B

What Is the Reformed Faith?

"The Reformed faith"[1] can be defined as a theology that describes and explains the sovereign God's revelation of His actions in history to glorify Himself by redeeming selected men and women from the just consequences of their self-inflicted depravity.

It is first and foremost *theology* (the study of God), not *anthropology* (the study of humanity). Reformed thinking concentrates on developing a true knowledge of God that serves as the necessary context for all other knowledge. It affirms that the created world, including humanity itself, cannot be accurately understood apart from its relationship with the Creator.

The Reformed faith describes and explains God's revelation of Himself and His actions to humanity; it does not consist of people's attempts to define God as they wish. The Reformed faith asserts that God has revealed Himself in two distinct ways. He reveals His existence, wisdom, and power through the created universe—a process known as *natural revelation* (Romans 1:18–32); and He reveals His requirements and plans for mankind through His written Word, the Bible—a process known as *special revelation* (2 Timothy 3:16–17).

Reformed theologians uphold the Bible as the inspired, infallible, inerrant, authoritative, and fully sufficient communication of truth from God to us. When they say the Bible is "inspired," they mean that the Bible was actually written by God through the agency of human authorship in a miraculous way that preserved the thoughts of God from any taint of human sinfulness (2 Peter 1:20–21).

When they say the Bible is infallible, they mean it is *incapable* of error, and when they say it is inerrant, they mean the Bible, *in actual fact,* contains no errors. The Bible is authoritative because it comes from God whose authority over His creation is absolute (Isaiah 46:9–10). And it is completely sufficient because it contains everything necessary for us to know and live according to God's requirements (2 Peter 1:3–4).

By studying God's revelation of Himself and His work, Reformed theologians have learned two foundational truths that structure their thinking about God's relationship with human beings: God is absolutely sovereign, and people are totally depraved.[2]

Reformed thought affirms that God, by definition, is *absolutely sovereign*—that is, He controls and superintends every circumstance of life either by direct miraculous intervention or by the ordinary outworking of His providence. Reformed theologians understand that a "god" who is not sovereign cannot be God because his power would not be absolute. Since the Reformed faith accepts the Bible's teaching regarding the sovereignty of God, it denies that *anything* occurs outside of God's control.

The Reformed faith affirms the biblical teaching that Adam was created with the ability to sin and chose to do so by disobeying a clear command of God (Genesis 3:1–7). Choosing to sin changed basic human nature and left us unable not to sin—or *totally depraved.* Total depravity does not mean that all people are as bad as they possibly could be, but that every facet of their character is tainted with sin, leaving them incapable and undesirous of fellowship with God. The Reformed faith denies that totally depraved men and women have any ability to seek after or submit to God of their own free will. Left to themselves, totally depraved men and women will remain out of fellowship with God for all eternity.

The only way for any of these men and women to have their fellowship with God restored is for God Himself to take the initiative. And the Bible declares that He has graciously chosen to do so (John 14:16). *For His own glory,* God has chosen some of those depraved men and women to live in fellowship with Him. His choice is determined by His own good pleasure and not by any virtue in the ones He has chosen. For this reason, *grace* is defined in Reformed thought as "unmerited favor."

God accomplished the salvation of His chosen ones by sending His Son, the Lord Jesus Christ, to bear God's righteous wrath against sin so that He could forgive those He had chosen. Even though Christ's work was perfect and complete, its effectiveness is limited to those who are chosen by God for salvation. Christ would not have been required to suffer any more or any less had a different number been chosen for redemption, but the benefit of His suffering is applied only to those who are called by God to believe in Him.

All of those who are thus effectually called by God will eventually believe and be saved, even though they may resist for a time (John 6:37). They cannot forfeit the salvation they have received (John 10:27–30; Romans 8:31–39).

Reformed thought affirms the clear teaching of the Bible that salvation is by faith alone through Christ alone (John 14:6; Acts 4:12; Ephesians 2:8–9), and that our good works play no part in salvation although they are generated by it (Ephesians 2:10). Salvation transforms a person's nature, giving him or her the ability and the desire to serve and obey God. The unresponsive heart of stone is changed into a sensitive heart of flesh that responds readily to God's voice (Ezekiel 36:25–27) and desires to glorify Him out of gratitude for the indescribable gift of salvation.

Reformed thought affirms that *God works in history to redeem* His chosen ones through a series of covenants. These covenants define His law, assess penalties for breaking His law, and provide for the imputation of Jesus' vicarious fulfillment of God's requirements to those God intends to redeem.[3]

The Reformed faith affirms that we were created and exist solely to glorify God, and denies that God exists to serve us. It affirms that God acts to glorify Himself by putting His attributes on display, and that His self-glorifying actions are thoroughly righteous since He is the only Being in creation worthy of glorification. It denies that God is *primarily* motivated to act by man's needs, but affirms that all of God's actions are motivated *primarily* for His own glory.

The Reformed faith emerged as a distinct belief system during the sixteenth and seventeenth centuries when men like Luther, Calvin, Zwingli, and Knox fought against the Roman Catholic

Church to restore Christian doctrine to biblical truth. These men were labeled "Reformers," but they would have been better labeled "Restorers" since their goal was to correct abuses and distortions of Christianity that were rampant in the established Roman church. Reformed thinkers since their day have sought to align their understanding of God and His actions in history as closely as possible to His revealed truth.

Notes

1. This brief overview of basic Reformed beliefs is not intended to be a full explanation of or apologetic for the Reformed faith. For a more detailed description and analysis of the Reformed faith see: R. C. Sproul, *Grace Unknown* (Grand Rapids: Baker, 1997), Loraine Boettner, *The Reformed Faith* (Phillipsburg, N.J.: Presbyterian and Reformed, 1983), *Back to Basics: Rediscovering the Richness of the Reformed Faith,* ed. David G. Hagopian (Phillipsburg, N.J.: P&R Publishing, 1996), *The Westminster Confession of Faith* (with its accompanying catechisms), or the theological writings of John Calvin, B. B. Warfield, Charles Hodge, and Louis Berkhof.

2. Both of these truths are taught throughout the pages of Scripture; however, the sovereignty of God can be seen very clearly in Isaiah 40–60 and in Job 38–42, while human depravity is described quite graphically in Romans 3:10–18.

3. An excellent discussion of these covenants is contained in chapter 5 of R. C. Sproul, *Grace Unknown.*

Map of the Holy Land

This blank map is for your use in a number of exercises that call for locating and marking key places in the life of Christ.

Recommended Reading

Boice, James Montgomery. *The Christ of Christmas.* Chicago: Moody Press, 1983.

Bruce, A. B. *The Training of the Twelve.* Grand Rapids: Kregel, 1971, 1988.

DeGraaf, S. G. *Promise and Deliverance.* 4 vols. Translated by H. Evan Runner and Elisabeth Wichers Runner. St Catharines, Ontario, Canada: Paideia Press, 1981.

Edersheim, Alfred. *The Life and Times of Jesus the Messiah.* McLean, Va.: MacDonald, n.d.

Guthrie, Donald. *Jesus the Messiah.* Grand Rapids: Zondervan, 1972.

Henry, Carl F. H. *The Identity of Jesus of Nazareth.* Nashville, Tenn.: Broadman Press, 1992.

Lloyd-Jones, D. Martyn. *Studies in the Sermon on the Mount.* Grand Rapids: Eerdmans, 1959-60.

MacArthur, John, Jr. *The Legacy of Jesus.* Chicago: Moody Press, 1986.

McDowell, Josh, *The Resurrection Factor.* San Bernardino, Calif.: Here's Life, 1981.

Morison, Frank. *Who Moved the Stone?* Downers Grove, Ill.: InterVarsity Press, n.d.

Rainsford, Marcus. *Our Lord Prays for His Own.* Grand Rapids: Kregel, 1950, 1978, 1985.

Sproul, R. C. *The Glory of Christ.* Wheaton, Ill.: Tyndale House, 1990.

Spurgeon, C. H. *Christ in the Old Testament*. 1899. Reprint Chattanooga, Tenn.: AMG Publishers, 1994.

Warfield, Benjamin Breckinridge. *The Person and Work of Christ*. Edited by Samuel G. Craig. Philadelphia: Presbyterian and Reformed, 1950.